INFLATION WEALTH GENERATOR

Harness Inflation and Supercharge Your Net Worth

ROGER MARTINEZ

Table of Contents

Disclaimer

The information provided in this book is for general informational purposes only and should not be considered as professional financial advice. The author is not a licensed financial advisor or accountant and does not guarantee the accuracy, completeness or reliability of any information provided.

The opinions expressed in this book regarding strategies and forecasts are solely those of the author and may turn out to be incorrect. None of the strategies discussed should be regarded as recommendations. The author cannot accurately predict future events, including but not limited to the price of gold, silver, real estate, stock and bond market conditions, future inflation or interest rates, or the likelihood of a monetary crisis. Therefore, it is not advisable to make financial decisions based on these forecasts.

The reader is responsible for their own financial decisions and should consult with a licensed professional before making any financial decisions. The author and publisher are not responsible for any actions taken by the reader as a result of reading this book.

Any examples, case studies or thought experiments presented in this book are for illustrative purposes only and should not be considered as a guarantee of financial success. Results may vary depending on individual circumstances and market conditions.

Finally, the reader should be aware that investing and personal finance involve risk, and past performance is not indicative of future results. The reader should do their own research and due diligence before making any investment decisions.

Inflation ... is the increase in the volume of money and bank credit in relation to the volume of goods. It is harmful because it depreciates the value of the monetary unit, raises everybody's cost of living, imposes what is in effect a tax on the poorest (without exemptions) at as high a rate as the tax on the richest, wipes out the value of past savings, discourages future savings, redistributes wealth and income wantonly, encourages and rewards speculation and gambling at the expense of thrift and work, undermines confidence in the justice of a free enterprise system, and corrupts public and private morals. But it is never "inevitable." We can always stop it overnight, if we have the sincere will to do so.

– Henry Hazlitt,
What you Should Know About Inflation, 1964

Introduction

Congratulations! You're going to be a millionaire. Maybe even a multimillionaire. The bad news ... by the time it happens the average SUV will cost a million dollars. Same with a college education. A house? Well, you don't want to know how many millions of dollars that will cost in the future.

The specter of high inflation is scary. Even if you don't understand what it is or where it comes from, you know it's one of the worst things that can happen to your finances.

You've probably seen those old-time photographs from the early 1920s of the hyperinflation of Weimar Republic of Germany, when prices doubled every 3.7 days. The ones showing harried Germans rushing to and fro, pushing wheelbarrows full of billions of worthless paper marks. Trying to spend the currency as fast as they could before it lost even more value.

You've probably heard recent news reports about how the citizens of Argentina or Venezuela struggle to live with soaring prices caused by annual inflation rates in the triple figures. And recently, as inflation has suddenly spiked to nearly 8 percent in the USA after four decades of bubbling along at around 2 percent, you've seen for yourself how inflation can disrupt the entire economy and spike the prices you pay for your bacon, eggs and rent.

The standard definition of inflation that floats around the Internet is as dry as an economics text: "A general increase in the prices of goods and services in an economy. When the general price level rises, each unit of currency buys fewer goods and services; consequently, inflation corresponds to a reduction in the purchasing power of money."

That's a straightforward definition. But I prefer to think of inflation as more like a dangerous man-made monster – a cross between Frankenstein and Dracula that sucks the lifeblood out of the economy, hurts millions of innocent people and never really dies.

But seriously, inflation is no joke. It erodes and destroys the wealth of poor and rich equally, but it also benefits some people at the expense of others. It allows governments to spend more money than they should on foreign wars and misguided social welfare programs. And it ruthlessly destroys currencies.

In fact, the United States inflation has been steadily eating away at the value of the dollar for more than a century. Since the creation of the Federal Reserve in 1913, it has destroyed the purchasing power of our currency by approximately 97%. That means when Woodrow Wilson was just starting his presidency, three American copper pennies would buy what a $1 bill buys today. To put it another way, it takes $30.20 in 2023 dollars to buy what a single silver dollar bought in 1913.

As an American I mourn this steep decline in the dollar's value, but all the world's currencies are in similar trouble. Inflation is a global scourge. Whether you trade in euros, yuan, yen, pesos, rupees or any of the 176 other currencies currently in circulation around the world, it is eroding your purchasing power and wealth. Unfortunately, the omnipresence of inflation makes the lessons of this book applicable – and valuable – to readers of every nation.

Would we and the world be better off with sound money and stable prices and maybe even, gasp, mild deflation? Absolutely. But for the time being we live in an inflationary world, and there is nothing you or I can do about it.

However, I believe we owe a duty to ourselves, our families and our country to preserve, grow and protect our wealth from those who would take it from us. I wrote this book to show ordinary people and investors how they can accomplish these things by harnessing the power of inflation. It contains many practical tips and a lot of sound financial advice about how to take advantage of what I call "Inflation Wealth Generators," but it also reveals two important secrets you should never forget.

The first secret is that inflation is a tax. Other than the occasional supply shock that temporarily drives up the price of oil or coffee or baby formula, inflation is a government-made phenomenon imposed upon the populace by a government unwilling to honestly tax the private sector to pay for its spending.

However, since in the real world there is no such thing as a free lunch, we know that all government spending must be paid for by someone eventually. It is paid either by explicit taxation, like an income or sales tax, or through the hidden tax of inflation. And unlike the "progressive" income tax, the inflation tax is regressive and hurts the poor and middle class the most.

That leads us to this book's second big important secret -- that inflation transfers wealth from the poor and the middle class to the wealthy, from the saver to the debtor, and from the wage earner to the politically connected.

But this devious transfer process doesn't necessarily have to harm you. Many fortunes have been made during times of financial crisis. And as I show you in the following pages, the current crisis in our country is a great opportunity to use the power of inflation to transfer wealth and purchasing power to you instead of someone else.

****

As much as anything, this book was written to be easily understood and fun to read. Chapters 1, 2 and 3 are an introduction to the basics of the money supply and the devilish nature of inflation – what it is, why we have it and the harmful effects it has on the economy, the purchasing power of the dollar and our personal finances. These chapters provide a foundation for our later discussion of investment strategies that you can put into action.

Chapter 4 shows how a little forethought and planning can make it easy to protect your wealth from the worst that high inflation can bring you.

Chapter 5 explains how you can "hedge against inflation" by converting your dollars into real assets that will preserve or even grow your wealth during periods of high inflation.

Chapter 6 explains how you can use inflation to generate new wealth for yourself by borrowing money and investing it in assets that will hold their value over time.

Chapter 7 focuses on the King of All Inflation Wealth Generators – the fixed-rate home mortgage, which millions of people from all income levels have greatly benefited from for almost a century without realizing it.

Chapter 8 compares several fictional home mortgage scenarios to show how inflation and the wealth-creating power of a long-term mortgage reversed the fortunes of a man who was drowning in $4 million in debt.

Chapter 9 discusses Cash-Out Refinancing, Reverse Mortgages, and SBA loans as additional Inflation Wealth Generators.

Chapter 10 issues a warning about deflation, the worst thing that can go wrong when your investment strategy is based on the expectation of a prolonged period of high inflation.

Chapter 11 is a list of smaller destructive acts by federal and local government that can jeopardize the success of our near-perfect Inflation Wealth Generator, the fixed-rate home mortgage.

And Chapter 12 is a look at the future and a recap of the things you should do and not do to safeguard your wealth and purchasing power in a time of high inflation.

What is notably missing from this book is a discussion of the plusses and minuses of cryptocurrencies. Let me start by saying that despite the serious decline of crypto prices and the bankruptcy of FTX in the fall of 2022, I hope crypto is a huge success and becomes the reserve currency of the monetary system.

I also hope that everyone who has invested in crypto becomes rich beyond their wildest dreams. But since coming into existence a mere 13 years ago, crypto's track record is too short for me to recommend it as an inflation hedge.

Not to worry, though. My book is filled with much tried and tested financial advice so that anyone of ordinary means can generate a fortune by harnessing the winds of inflation instead of being flattened by them.

I have been a student of inflation since the bailouts of the 2008 Financial Crisis and I've studied nearly every book, podcast, interview and news article on the subject. But I have yet to come across an easily understandable book that offered practical advice for beating inflation.

I wrote this book with the average investor in mind, not Warren Buffet or someone who swaps derivatives for a living. But why should you trust me, a medical doctor, to give you investment advice?

It's not because I have an economics degree from Stanford University. Though my courses there provided me with a solid understanding of macroeconomic concepts, it was my real-world experience that has given me what amounts to a grad school education in finance and investing.

I have been investing in stocks for the last twenty-five years and in real estate for the last fifteen. The stock market has been good to me, but most of my financial success has come from residential and commercial real estate. I own multiple residential rental properties, have built a hotel and am in the process of building two more.

My investments allowed me to semi-retire in my early forties. As much as I would like to credit my success to my financial brilliance, it was inflation that actually did the hard work. I just hoisted the sails and let the steady winds of inflation carry me along. At times I hit the rocks, as you will read about later. But for the most part, and in the long run, it has been a rewarding voyage. It's my hope that I can show you too how to get rich by harnessing the power of inflation.

Chapter 1

What is Inflation?

Inflation is when you pay fifteen dollars for the ten-dollar haircut you used to get for five dollars when you had hair.
– Sam Ewing

Most of us could not give the Econ 101 definition of inflation if our lives depended on it, but we know it when we see it:

That haircut that used to cost $5 now costs $15. Inflation. That pair of movie tickets, bucket of popcorn and two sodas that used to cost $30 now costs $75. Inflation.

And it's not just the luxuries or little extras that are costing us more every year. It's the prices of life's basic necessities that have risen the most. Perhaps you recently experienced the pain of inflation firsthand when your landlord gave notice that your rent is increasing by $300 a month.

Or when they raised your health care premium 25%. Or maybe you finally realized there's a serious inflation problem when the college education that your grandfather paid for by working part-time summer jobs now costs you a student loan the size of a McMansion mortgage.

Inflation. Inflation. Inflation. It's not good. It's everywhere. But what is it?

Technically defined, inflation means the expansion of the supply of money. If the supply of goods and services fails to keep up with the expansion of the money supply, it leads to rising prices. This is because there are more dollars chasing the same amount of goods and services.

Materially, that means dollars have lost value because they can buy less food or fewer haircuts than they did before. In everyday language, and in the media, inflation means rising prices. Going forward, we will use inflation and rising prices interchangeably.

Let's look at a simplified example of how expanding the money supply leads to rising prices. Say you and nine of your friends are attending an auction for 10 identical widgets at Bubba's Auction House.

Bubba, the auctioneer, has given each of you 1 token to bid with. The tokens are only good at Bubba's Auction House and can only be used for today's auction. Since ten people have 1 token each, the total "money supply" at Bubba's is 10 tokens. If there are 10 widgets and 10 tokens, then the average price per widget will be 1 token. Pretty straightforward right?

But then Bubba offers a special promotion. Because of your loyal patronage, he is giving each of you an additional token to bid with. You and your friends let out excited hoots and give each other high fives and back slaps. You are all twice as rich. Yay!

Now each of you has 2 tokens and the total money supply at the auction has doubled to 20 tokens. But here's the kicker. Bubba doubled the money supply, but he did not double the supply of widgets for sale. Once all the excitement of receiving an extra token has died down, you realize that you are not twice as rich after all.

That's because the average price per widget will now be 2 tokens. Each of your tokens is now worth half as much as it used to be. One token used to buy one widget, but now it takes two tokens to buy that exact same widget. The price of a widget at Bubba's Auction House has doubled. Or to put it another way, inflation of the token supply at Bubba's cut the purchasing power of your token in half.

The exact same thing that happened at Bubba's – the devaluation of the currency -- happens to an entire economy when the government inflates the money supply. Prices go up. The government can print more and more dollar bills, but it cannot print more houses, food, cars, doctors, etc. So the ever-increasing number of dollars chasing the same amount of goods and services inevitably leads to higher prices. Inflation.

Now the media, academia and politicians delight in blaming inflation on greedy corporations, slumlords, stock speculators, middlemen, or whatever capitalist villain du jour the public loves to hate. But greedy capitalists are victims of inflation just like everyone else. Their labor costs, rent, supplies and taxes are rising just as fast for them as for the rest of us. So who or what is causing inflation? Well, I hate to tell you this, but look in the mirror -- it's you.

I know what you are thinking. "I work for wages and I'm living paycheck to paycheck. I'm the little guy. How could I possibly be responsible for inflation?

Well, do you vote? Then you've probably helped to elect some of the bums in Congress and the White House who have increased the national debt every year since the Calvin Coolidge administration. Republicans or Democrats, it doesn't matter. Republicans, those supposed stalwarts of fiscal discipline, have been just as bad or worse than the Democrats. Ronald Reagan increased the national debt by 186% and George W. Bush by 105%.

Even if you did not vote, however, you're just as guilty because you shirked your civic duty and allowed these big-spending politicians to get elected and re-elected. If you are too young to vote or if you consistently voted for a third party that had a balanced budget in their platform, then you get a pass. As for the rest of us, we are almost as guilty as the politicians we've sent to Washington, DC. Almost.

The national debt at the writing of this book is $31 trillion, which equals $97,000 per citizen. That's bad, but it's actually much worse than that. Not every American will be able to help pay back the debt. Most citizens are net tax recipients. Meaning that they receive more in government benefits than they contribute in taxes. We cannot expect them to help pay back the debt in the future when they are not even self-sufficient in the present. When we remove millions of children, retirees and citizens living on welfare and Social Security, and only consider current net taxpayers, the debt obligation per citizen nearly doubles to $167,000.

That is a big number. That's a down payment on a beautiful house in a great school district. But wait... it gets worse. When we take into consideration all the state and local government debt, student loan debt and unfunded liabilities, etc., that national debt number grows to well over $1 million per net taxpayer. Do you have $1 million lying around to bail out the government? I didn't think so.

You might be wondering, "How did this happen? Where were the grownups? How did our elected officials let things get so bad? And what the heck does this have to do with inflation?"

Well, it is pretty simple. Politicians like to get elected and reelected. And voters like free stuff. It was not long before politicians figured out they could buy votes by bribing voters with free government stuff and voters figured out they could get that free government stuff by electing politicians willing to plunder the national treasury for it.

And let's be honest, there are not many among us who would turn our noses up at free healthcare, free retirement, free education, free food, free rent, free smart phones, etc. But that's the thing. They are not free. Not really. They might be free to the recipients, but someone has to pay for that free stuff. But who? Again, I hate to tell you this, but it's you.

You're probably thinking, "Tell me something I don't know. Of course, I'm paying for government spending. I pay federal and state income taxes, property tax, sales tax, capital gains tax, etc."

That's all true, but what you probably don't know is that at the same time you're paying those taxes you and everybody else are also paying an unseen tax. A secret tax.

In the past, when we were on a gold standard, the government could not just print up a new pile of paper money to spend. In theory at least, when an ounce of gold was set at $35 an ounce, the government had to obtain 1/35th ounces of gold whenever it issued a new dollar bill. The dollar bill in your pocket was basically a vault receipt that you could redeem for 1/35th ounce of gold. If the federal government wanted to spend tens of billions of dollars on a social program or a war, it either had to find more gold, plunder another nation, borrow the money, or tax its own citizens.

The trouble is, gold is really hard to find, and when you do find it, it is dangerous and expensive to extract. The same goes with invading another country. Fighting a war is extremely costly in treasure and lives, and contrary to popular sentiment, it's rarely a profitable endeavor.

So, if the government cannot find more gold or steal more money from somewhere to pay for its spending, then taxation and borrowing are the only options left. Did I forget to mention that voters really hate paying taxes? On the one hand, voters really love getting those government goodies; on the other hand, they really hate having to pay for them. And campaigning on a platform of tax hikes is, or at least it used to be, a guaranteed losing strategy for any politician.

So what is an ambitious politician who wants to get elected and reelected to do? Borrow money by the trillions, of course -- hence our enormous national debt. And what they can't borrow from other countries' central banks, private individuals, or corporations, they will borrow from the Federal Reserve who simply prints the money it lends.

All government debt and spending must be paid back with taxes eventually. But luckily for politicians, there is a tax that can be levied on citizens without their knowledge or consent. It is omnipresent, relentless and it taxes the rich, middle class and poor alike. It taxes both the money in a child's piggy bank and a retiree's pension. It even skims the ill-gotten gains of the drug dealer, con man and pimp.

The beauty of this tax, from the politician's perspective, is that the taxpayers don't even realize they are paying a tax. Public confusion surrounding this tax is so pervasive that politicians who impose it escape blame and are able actively rail against it.

This politically perfect tax is called, you guessed it, inflation. Politicians print excess dollars to fund their spending without directly taxing the citizens. It is this inflation of the money supply that causes prices to rise.

And that's it. That's the big secret. Inflation is really a tax. If you understand that, then you know more than 99% of the population. You were never supposed to learn that inflation is a tax. But it is true. The difference between the inflated price of something and the price absent inflation is the tax.

But there is an even bigger secret about inflation that the people running the world do not want you to know. A secret that the politicians and the rich have carefully kept to themselves. A secret that you can quickly understand. A secret that you can easily use to your financial advantage.

That secret knowledge is the premise of this book. Simply

stated, it is: inflation transfers wealth from everyone who saves, loans or gets paid in dollars to those who have debts priced in dollars. To state it even more simply: inflation transfers wealth from savers to debtors.

Anti-climactic? Maybe. Too simple? I prefer elegant.

The Federal Reserve has a target of 2% inflation a year. That is its official policy – or it was until inflation spiked above 8 percent in 2022. The Fed has told us to our faces that it wants to devalue the dollar by 2% a year. Why? Well, we know inflation redistributes wealth to debtors. And who is the biggest debtor in the history of the world? Answer: The U.S. federal government. Now you should understand why inflation creation is official policy.

We have three very valuable pieces of information about inflation to review:

1. Inflation redistributes wealth from savers to debtors.
2. The U.S. federal government is the biggest debtor in the history of the world.
3. The official policy of the Federal Reserve is to create inflation.

Before we get into explaining how inflation transfers wealth from savers to debtors, we'll examine how the dollar has value despite not being backed by anything tangible.

Once we understand where the dollar gets its value, then we will understand how the government can – at least in the short run – get away with printing an unlimited amount of them. More important, then we'll learn how knowing how the government's inflation racket works can make you rich.

Chapter 2

Why the Dollar Has Value and Why We have Inflation

"Political power grows out of the barrel of a gun."
—Mao Zedong

Have you ever wondered why the dollar has value? If you are like most people, the thought has probably never crossed your mind. You have always accepted these little green pieces of paper in exchange for your time and labor and take for granted that you can exchange dollars for just about anything you want or need. But why? What gives the dollar its value?

A lot of people think that it's because the dollar is backed by gold. It is not. We have been completely off the gold standard for over 50 years. Its value is backed up by the immense power of the federal government. The dollar is what we call a fiat currency. This type of currency has value, not because it has intrinsic value or is backed by something like gold, but because a powerful person like a king or president says it does.

In the case of the United States, the federal government has decreed that dollars are legal tender. This means that the government will accept dollars as payment for your tax obligations. So, if you have enough dollars to pay your tax bill, then the government will not throw you in jail. Therein lies the ultimate value of the dollar – if you have enough of them, you can avoid governmental violence.

That is the bonus secret of this book: both the dollar's value and the government's power are derived from the threat of violence. If you understand that, then you know more than 99.9% of the population. But it's best to keep this secret to yourself. Informing patriotic people that the basis of their government's power is the threat of violence will not be appreciated.

In fact, this probably comes as quite a shock to you. You probably thought the value of the dollar derives from our nation's military and economic might, the productivity and entrepreneurial spirit of the American people, or the dollar's status as a global reserve currency. There is some truth to all of that, but in the end the dollar has value because the guys with the guns tell us it does.

Don't believe me? Try paying your taxes in sea shells or wampum. Better yet, don't pay them at all and let me know what happens. Spoiler alert! If you persist long enough, large men with guns will drag you out of your house and throw you in a cage. If you resist, they will kill you. Sounds crazy, right? But ask yourself. If the US government laid down all its arms today and made taxes voluntary, would the dollar have value tomorrow? In that same scenario, what would happen to gold's value?

Still skeptical? Let us look at a simple scenario that illustrates how force or even just the threat of force creates value for a fiat currency. Suppose there is a schoolyard bully named Dirk. Now Dirk is a real jerk. He is bigger and meaner than all the other kids, and what he says goes. If you complained about something he did, he would hit you so hard you'd never complain again. Even the teachers are afraid of him.

Dirk has a problem. It is exhausting having to constantly beat people up to steal their stuff or get them to do your bidding. On occasion, he might even bruise his knuckles on some poor nerd's face.

But then Dirk, being a bright and ambitious young autocrat, comes up with an elegant solution for fleecing his subjects. One that did not require the constant pummeling of his victims. He starts printing Dirk Dollars. He distributes some of the Dirk Dollars to his entourage of toadies and sycophants and keeps the rest for himself.

Now Dirk Dollars are nothing special. They are not lined in gold or adorned with beautiful artwork. Dirk just prints them on regular paper from his home computer. What gives them value is that if you can present Dirk with a Dirk Dollar whenever he asks (taxes), then he leaves you alone. Oh sure, he might give you a titty twister or a noogie just to remind you who is boss, but for the most part he lets you go in peace. On the flipside, if you cannot produce a Dirk Dollar when Dirk comes calling, he throws you a beating (jailtime).

It is obvious here why Dirk Dollars have value. If you have a Dirk Dollar, you avoid the beating. There is great value in not getting assaulted. Consequently, you are willing to trade for Dirk Dollars just to avoid the pummeling. Maybe you would trade your lunch for a Dirk Dollar. Maybe you would be willing to do someone's homework for a Dirk Dollar.

The reverse is also true. If you have surplus Dirk Dollars, then you could buy someone's lunch with them or pay someone to do your homework. The Dirk Dollars can have value beyond just escaping the bully's drubbing. The same is true of the US dollar. Its value extends beyond merely allowing you to escape the taxman's wrath.

When Dirk wants more currency, he just prints Dirk Dollars. Unlike Dirk, the U.S. federal government cannot print dollars, or at least it must avoid the appearance that it is simply printing dollars. It has to jump through some ceremonial hoops first.

Fiat currencies depend on confidence. If people think the government is just printing funny money at will, they will refuse to transact in it and its value can go to zero even with the looming threat of government force.

When the United States was making the long transition away from the gold standard, to reassure the public, checks were put into the financial system in an attempt to at least avoid the appearance that it is doing exactly what it is -- simply printing money.

The United States has run a deficit every year since 1970 except during the dotcom bubble of 1998-2001. That means when the federal government needs more dollars in excess of tax revenues to pay for social programs or national defense it must borrow the dollars. It issues bonds, Treasury Bills (T-Bills) that it is obligated to pay back. Hence our $32 trillion national debt.

Confused? Well, that's kind of the point. How the federal government actually manages the money supply is very complicated and it's meant to obscure the fact that the government is for all practical purposes just printing money. Understanding the process is not necessary for our purposes. All we need to know is that if the government wants more dollars, it can conjure them into existence. If you're interested in how the sausage is managed, I recommend watching Mike Maloney's "Hidden Secrets of Money" series, Episode 5.

Meanwhile, let's get back to our bully Dirk. He created Dirk Dollars so that he could buy goods and services with no effort on his part except for intimidating his victims. This is true of all creators of fiat money, including counterfeiters. Governments print new dollars so they can consume resources without having to pay for them. The problem arises when governments create too much currency and there is too much currency chasing too few goods and services.

As we saw at Bubba's Auction House, this leads to inflation.

But at least Bubba gave everyone an extra token at the same time he doubled the price of a widget. In real life, the financial and political elites get the newly printed government dollars first -- before the prices of goods and services rise. Everyone else just gets the higher prices.

Summary

- [ ] Fiat currencies derive their value from the issuing government's ability to impose taxes by force if necessary.
- [ ] The U.S. dollar, aka Federal Reserve Note, and every other contemporary currency in the world are fiat currencies.
- [ ] There is a great temptation for issuers of fiat currency – governments – to over-inflate their money supply, leading to higher prices.
- [ ] The Wall Street and K Street elites receive the newly printed dollars before prices rise. Main Street gets them after the prices have already risen.

Inflation Redistributes Wealth

As stated above, to get elected and reelected, politicians have a strong incentive to spend money on favored projects and goodies for preferred voting blocs. They also have a strong incentive to not raise taxes to pay for this high level of spending. Predictably, they print money, which results in too many dollars chasing too few goods, which leads to increasing prices. What is much less commonly known is that inflation transfers wealth from one group of citizens to another. Inflation does not necessarily destroy wealth, but it redistributes it.

We stated earlier that inflation transfers wealth from savers, creditors and people on a fixed income to debtors, but how? Before we explain, we must define the following terms that are essential in discussing and understanding the phenomenon of inflation:

> **Nominal interest rate** – is the interest rate without adjusting for inflation. Nominal interest rate is usually just called "the interest rate." When someone says their home mortgage has a 4% interest rate, it is the same as saying that their home mortgage has a nominal interest rate of 4%.
>
> **Real Interest rate** – adjusts for inflation by subtracting the inflation rate from the nominal interest rate, and can be described by the following equation:
>
> **Real Interest Rate = Nominal Interest Rate – Inflation Rate**

For example, if your mortgage interest rate is 4% and the inflation rate is 1% then the real interest rate of your mortgage is 3%. Real interest rates can even be negative. For example, if your mortgage interest rate is 4% and the inflation rate is 5%, then the real interest rate is –1%.

> **Purchasing Power** – the value of goods and services that a unit of currency can buy. Over time inflation decreases the purchasing power of a given unit of currency. If annual inflation is running at 10 percent, the dollar in your pocket right now will buy only 91 cents worth of goods and services a year from now.

Simply put, when real interest rates turn negative, wealth is transferred from creditors to debtors – from the people who have money to lend to the people who borrow money. This is because the purchasing power of the cash loaned out today is more than the purchasing power of the principal and interest that will be paid back in the future. Or to put it another way, the loan will be paid off with dollars that can buy less stuff in the future than the original dollars loaned.

If you had a hard time understanding that last sentence, then you are like 99.9% of the human population since prehistoric times. We did not evolve to think in terms of interest and inflation rates. Our evolution was dictated by the external forces of the real world where 2 is always greater than 1. Our evolution was not influenced by the modern abstract concepts of economics and finance where the value of 2 relative to 1 depends on the interest rate, the inflation rate and length of the loan term.

But make no mistake, the political and financial elites understand the interplay between interest and inflation well – and they use it to enrich themselves at the expense of the unwitting public.

Inflation Compounds Exponentially

Albert Einstein called "compound interest" the eighth wonder of the world. When you save money in a bank, for example, the interest you earn on it each year is added to your principal (the original amount) and then you earn interest on your principal + interest. From then on you earn interest on your principal + interest + interest. It is a snowball effect and, before not too long, what you earn in interest each year is larger than the original amount you put in the bank.

This is called exponential growth – growth that increasingly increases. It is truly a miracle of wealth creation when it increases your savings and investments. But exponential growth is a nightmare when it increases your expenses, which is what happens during inflation.

The inflation rate is the rate that prices increase annually. The inflation rate works over time just like compounding interest does, only it causes prices to rise exponentially. In other words, inflation causes prices to increasingly increase. Let's look at an example that shows how "compound inflation" becomes a nightmare.

In April of 2022 the price of silver was approximately $25/ounce, so $100 bought 4 ounces of silver. Assume an annual inflation rate of 7%, and suppose the price of silver is perfectly correlated to inflation (i.e., if inflation is 7%, then the price of silver rises exactly 7% a year). If inflation holds steady at 7% for the next 100 years, the price of silver will double approximately every 10 years.

After the first decade, silver's price is $49.18 an ounce (Appendix: Table 1). Instead of being able to buy 4 ounces of silver with your $100 bill, you can now only buy 2 ounces. Inflation has cut the purchasing power of your dollars nearly in half. At year 21, the price of an ounce of silver more than doubles again to $103.51, so $100 won't even buy you 1 ounce of silver (Appendix: Table 1).

Between the years 40 and 41, inflation adds $26.21 to the price of an ounce – more than its original price of $25/ounce. At year 80, the price of silver hits an inflection point and increases nearly $1,000/year (Graph 1). After a hundred years, the price tops out at $21,692.91 an ounce.

Graph 1

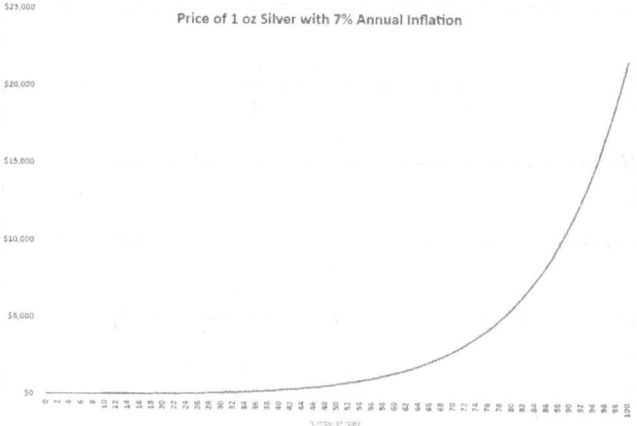

· 32 ·

Graph 2 flips the process around and demonstrates how a century's worth of 7% annual inflation massively devalues your $100 bill. The curve of Graph 2 represents the amount of silver that can be purchased with $100. The slope of the curve is steepest initially and then flattens out over time. This also shows that the rate of dollar devaluation is also greatest immediately and then levels off.

Initially, your $100 bill could buy 4 ounces of silver and after 4 years only 3 ounces. But after 10 years of 7% inflation per year $100 could only buy 2 ounces of silver and by year 21 it has been devalued to a level where it cannot purchase an additional ounce of silver. (See Appendix: Table 2)

Graph 2

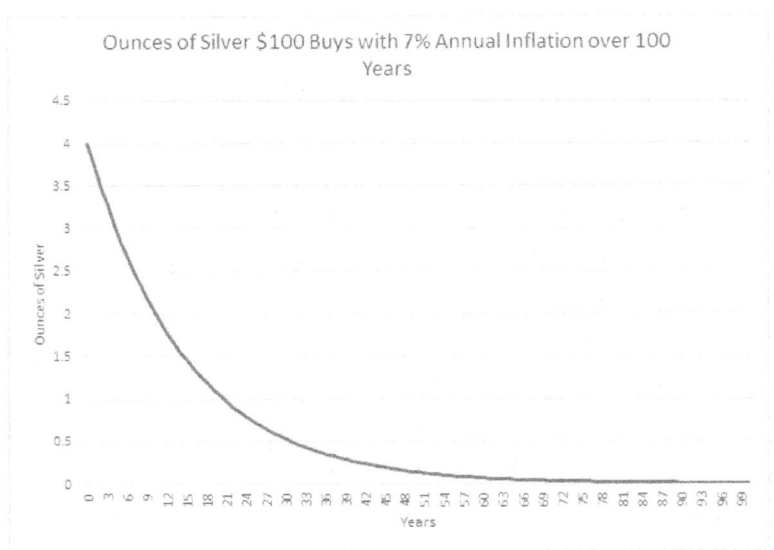

The rate of the dollar's devaluation decreases at a decreasing rate, or what mathematicians call "exponential decay." This is the reverse of the rising price of silver, which increases exponentially each year as seen in Graph 1. This is exactly what we would expect since the two graphs are illustrating the same event but from opposite perspectives. This will become important later as we discuss how to maximize our wealth from inflation.

This example of the devaluation of the dollar vis-à-vis silver assumes a relatively high and constant rate of inflation. That is a best-case scenario because a constant rate of inflation allows us to predict, plan and acclimate to it. Unfortunately, the coming era of inflation will most likely be unpredictable with intermittent bouts of inflation and deflation at varying rates accompanied by the simultaneous social and political upheaval common during financial crises.

Our best hope for a better and happier financial future is to find solid inflation hedges that will both preserve and grow our wealth. An inflation hedge is an asset or investment that protects our wealth from inflation. An inflation hedge must be positively correlated to inflation so that when inflation rises, then the price of the hedge also rises. Perfect correlation means for every percent rise in inflation there is a simultaneous exact rise in the price of the hedge.

Ideally, we want the price of our hedge to rise at an even greater rate than inflation so that it increases our purchasing power. Ideally, we also want a hedge that has minimal negative-tax consequences. After all, there's no point in having a hedge if the government is going to grab all your gains. Believe it or not, some inflation hedges are actually tax deductible. More on that happy thought later. For now, the next chapter will illustrate how important it is for you to pick the right inflation hedges.

Chapter 3

Meet Dr. Frugal
and Dr. Spendthrift

All you ants do is work all day. You should be
more like me and play, play, play!
– said the grasshopper to the ant

To further help us choose the right inflation hedge, let's examine the financial lives of Dr. Frugal and Dr. Spendthrift. They are two successful fictional physicians who both work at the same hospital but have very different investing styles.

For the sake of simplicity, we are assuming that their mortgages are non-amortizing and that the value of their assets (real estate, stocks, silver coins, etc.) rise at the exact same rate as inflation. We also assume that any stocks they own do not pay dividends. They make $500,000/year by working 2000 hours at $250/hr. As per their employment contract, they get a cost-of-living adjustment every year at the exact rate of inflation.

Meet Dr. Frugal

Dr. Frugal is a 35-year-old physician who has always been financially prudent. Despite his $500,000 annual income, he lives a modest lifestyle and is careful not to overspend. His wife is even more frugal than he is. They rarely eat out and vacations are spent camping in the nearby national forest. He plans on retiring in 30 years so he has been steadfastly investing and paying down debt.

Dr. Frugal considers himself ahead of the game. He did splurge on a beautiful $1 million home for his family but after years of diligently making extra mortgage payments he now owns it free and clear. After years of reading personal finance books, he knows how important it is to be debt free. He has managed to sock away $1 million in a traditional IRA. He also has a $100,000 emergency fund stashed safely in a savings account earning 0.01% interest.

Meet Dr. Spendthrift

Dr. Spendthrift is also a 35-year-old physician and makes the same $500,000 annual income. He has always been prone to overspending. His wife is a beautiful, capricious woman who is even more financially irresponsible than he is. They do not cook and almost always dine out at fashionable restaurants. They belong to a high income and high spending peer group, and Dr. Spendthrift often feels pressured to spend on luxury items and experiences. To impress his big spending friends, he bought a $2 million home and two $1 million vacation condos in Hawaii and California.

Dr. Spendthrift is drowning in debt and can barely pay the interest on his loans. He has no equity in any of his properties and still owes $100,000 in student loans. His mortgages and student loan are all 30-year fixed-interest-only at a 7% annual percentage rate (APR) with a balance balloon principal payment due at the end of term. All told, Dr. Spendthrift is $4.1 million in debt requiring $287,000 in annual interest payments.

Dr. Spendthrift has no retirement account; he just has never gotten around to setting one up. His only asset is his silver coin collection, which is worth $100,000. At this point, Dr. Spendthrift cannot even contemplate retirement.

In fact, in 30 years when the balloon payments on his properties are due, barring a miracle, he fears that he will be left impoverished and homeless. He spends many sleepless nights fretting over his hopeless financial situation and worries if he'll get sick or otherwise be unable to work. Sometimes he secretly hopes that he dies so that at least his family might collect some life insurance.

Comparing their two balance sheets we see Dr. Frugal has a net worth of $3.1 million (Table 1) compared to Dr. Spendthrift's net worth of $0 (Table 2). If he desired, Dr. Frugal, with his prudent lifestyle, could opt to retire immediately. In contrast, Dr. Spendthrift is struggling. Despite years of earning a high income his net worth and retirement savings are zero. He has significantly underperformed his peers financially. At his current trajectory, Dr. Spendthrift will never be able to retire, much less in 30 years.

Dr. Frugal's Starting Balance Sheet
(Table 1)

Assets		Liabilities	
Primary Residence	$1,000,000	Mortgage	$0
Traditional IRA	$2,000,000		
Savings Account	$100,000		
Total Assets	$3,100,000	Total Liabilities	$0
Net Worth	$3,100,000		

Dr. Spendthrift's Starting Balance Sheet
(Table 2)

Assets		Liabilities	
Primary Residence	$2,000,000	Mortgage (Primary)	$2,000,000
Hawaii Vacation Home	$1,000,000	Mortgage (Hawaii)	$1,000,000
California Vacation Home	$1,000,000	Mortgage (California)	$1,000,000
Silver Coin Collection	$100,000	Student Loans	$100,000
Total Assets	$4,100,000	Total Liabilities	$4,100,000
Net Worth	$0		

It's obvious that our Dr. Frugal is in much better financial shape than Dr. Spendthrift. But what if over the next 30 years the country begins experiencing an average inflation rate of 10% per year?

That's only moderately high inflation. But in our fictitious scenario it caused some interesting -- and surprising -- things to happen to the finances of our pair of doctors as they traveled their starkly different roads to retirement.

The Story of Dr. Frugal

Luckily for Dr. Frugal and Dr. Spendthrift, their incomes exactly kept up with inflation. Although the amount of dollars they earned increased an average of 10% a year, the inflation rate of 10% devalued those dollars, and, as a result, their total pretax purchasing power remained the same.

Unfortunately, though, thanks to a phenomenon known

as "bracket creep," their after-tax purchasing power actually decreased. Bracket creep occurs when inflation lifts a taxpayer's income into a higher tax bracket. This results in a higher income tax obligation even though no increase in real income occurred. After-tax purchasing power is therefore decreased because the inflated income is taxed at a higher rate.

As the years passed, Dr. Frugal found it difficult to save and invest because he had to spend more and more of his money on consumption. His children's college educations and weddings were particularly exorbitant. Since he was paying a higher percentage of his income in taxes, his higher income did not keep up with rising prices and he was unable to continue to add to his retirement account.

Still, he was not overly concerned. His stock portfolio and home values continued to rise every year at the exact rate of inflation. Both increased in price by almost 1700% over 30 years! He was wealthier... at least on paper.

At the beginning of the 30-year period, Dr. Frugal had a net worth of $3.1 million (Table 1) compared to Dr. Spendthrift's net worth of $0 (Table 2). After an additional 30 years of Dr. Spendthrift's imprudent and lavish lifestyle, we would expect his net worth to turn negative, and the wealth disparity between the two physicians to be even larger. But the exact opposite happened.

On the surface Dr. Frugal appeared to do quite well. He started out in 2023 with a net worth of $3.1 million and after 30 years it increased to $52,448,606 (Table 3). Not bad. He increased his net worth 1691%. That would be great except that at the same time inflation increased by 10% each year — a total compounded increase of 1745%.

In other words, Dr. Frugal's net worth would have had to increase by 1745% just to preserve the same purchasing power he had in 2023. He didn't quite break even. Adjusted for inflation, his net worth in 2053 is $3,005,748 — a drop of $94,252 in his purchasing power compared to 30 years earlier.

For Dr. Frugal to break even, his net worth in 2053 would have to be $54,093,147 (2053 dollars). He was about $1,644,641 or 3% short. What happened? Well, unfortunately, his $100,000 bank savings account didn't have a chance to keep up with 10% annual inflation. It only paid a 0.01% interest rate, which resulted in a piddling $300 of interest after 30 years.

Thanks to inflation, his savings account's real interest rate was a negative 9.99% (0.01% - 10.00% = -9.99%). Every year inflation ate away at the real value of his savings. To keep up with three decades of inflation, his bank savings account needed to grow to $1,744,940, but it ended up being worth just $100,300. Adjusted for inflation his savings account had a purchasing power of only $5,731 (2023 dollars) To put this sad tale another way, after 30 years Dr. Frugal's savings account only retained less than 6% of the purchasing power it had at the start.

Here in Dr. Frugal's story you can plainly see the steady, quiet, destructive power of inflation. It consumed over 94% of his savings account, but it didn't destroy that wealth, it just transferred it. But where and to whom? As we will see, inflation transferred the wealth in Dr. Frugal's savings account to Dr. Spendthrift and other debtors.

Dr. Frugal's Starting and Ending Net Worth
after 30 Years of 10% Annual Inflation (Table 3)

Assets	2023	2053	Liabilities	2023	2053
Primary Residence	$1,000,000	$17,449,402	Mortgage	$0	$0
IRA	$2,000,000	$34,898,804			
Savings	$100,000	$100,300			
Total Assets	$3,100,000	$52,448,506	Total Liabilities	$0	$0
Initial Net Worth	$3,100,000				
Final Net Worth		$52,448,506			
Final Real Net Worth (in 2023 dollars)		$3,005,748			

Change in Real Net Worth = -$94,252

The Story of Dr. Spendthrift

In contrast to Dr. Frugal, over the next 30 years Dr. Spendthrift's financial situation improved significantly because his income rose with inflation but the size of his debt and the interest payments on it stayed the same. Like Dr. Frugal, because of bracket creep he was paying a higher percentage of his income at a higher tax rate (albeit lower than Dr. Frugal's because he was able to tax deduct the mortgage interest on his primary residence).

Although Dr. Spendthrift's income increased 10% each year in step with inflation, his debt obligations remained fixed. Therefore, his debt payments became a lower and lower percentage of his annual income. So every year his debt payments became more manageable.

Originally, most of Dr. Spendthrift's income was consumed by his debt and when that burden eased over the next 30 years, he was able to lead an even more extravagant lifestyle. He continued to not save or invest, and he never did get around to opening that retirement account.

Surprisingly, though, Dr. Spendthrift did exceptionally well during the 30-year period of 10% inflation. He started out with a net worth of $0 and ended up with a net worth of $67,442,548 (Table 4). He went from a broke underachiever to a multimillionaire in just 30 years — he ended up even wealthier than Dr. Frugal who had $3.1 million head start. How did he achieve such a remarkable turnaround?

Just like Dr. Frugal, Dr. Spendthrift's assets increased at the same rate of inflation for a total increase of 1745% over the 30-year period — from $4,100,000 to $71,542,548 (Table 4). Since the interest rate of his debt was fixed, and since he paid off the interest every month, his debt principal stayed even at $4.1 million.

Even though the $4.1 million debt remained the same over the 30 years, its inflation-adjusted value steadily decreased. That is to say, the purchasing power of the dollars he needed to pay off his debt had decreased in value by 94%. Dr. Spendthrift's debt had an initial real value in 2023 of $4.1 million, but after 30 years of 10% inflation its final real value had declined to $258,462 (Table 5). That was a $3,865,035 real decrease in Dr. Spendthrift's liabilities and subsequently a $3,865,035 real increase in his net worth. Remember, it is not how much you make that determines your net worth, it is how much you keep.

Did Dr. Spendthrift become a voracious saver and put in massive amounts of overtime at his practice? Nope. Did he spend hours upon hours poring over reams of market research resulting in sharp stock picks and windfall stock market gains? Nope — he didn't even have a 401(k).

Dr. Spendthrift's Starting and Ending Net Worth after 30 Years of 10% Annual Inflation (Table 4)

Assets	2023	2053	Liabilities	2023	2053
Primary Residence	$2,000,000	$34,898,804	Mortgage (Primary)	$2m	$2m
Hawaii home	$1,000,000	$17,449,402	Mortgage (Hawaii)	$1m	$1m
California Home	$1,000,000	$17,449,402	Mortgage (CA)	$1m	$1m
Coin Collection	$100,000	$1,744,940	Student Loans	$100k	$100k
Total Assets	$4,100,000	$71,542,548	Total Liabilities	$4.1m	$4.1m
Initial Net Worth	$0				
Final Net Worth		$67,442,548			
Final Real Net Worth (in 2023 dollars)		$3,865,035			

Change in Real Net Worth = $3,865,035

Dr. Spendthrift's Inflation Adjusted Change
in Debt Value (in 2023 Dollars) (Table 5)

Year	Debt Value (in 2023 Dollars)	Change in Value	Year	Debt Value (in 2023 Dollars)	Change in Value
2023	$4,100,000	-$372,727	2039	$892,279	-$ 81,116
2024	$3,727,273	-$338,843	2040	$811,163	-$ 73,742
2025	$3,388,430	-$308,039	2041	$737,421	-$ 67,038
2026	$3,080,391	-$280,036	2042	$670,383	-$ 60,944
2027	$2,800,355	-$254,578	2043	$609,439	-$ 55,404
2028	$2,545,777	-$231,434	2044	$554,035	-$ 50,367
2029	$2,314,343	-$210,395	2045	$503,668	-$ 45,788
2030	$2,103,948	-$191,268	2046	$457,880	-$ 41,625
2031	$1,912,680	-$173,880	2047	$416,255	-$ 37,841
2032	$1,738,800	-$158,073	2048	$ 378,414	-$ 34,401
2033	$1,580,727	-$143,702	2049	$ 344,012	-$ 31,274
2034	$1,437,025	-$130,639	2050	$312,739	-$ 28,431
2035	$1,306,386	-$118,762	2051	$284,308	-$ 25,846
2036	$1,187,624	-$107,966	2052	$258,462	-$ 23,497
2037	$1,079,658	-$ 98,151	2053	$234,965	
2038	$ 981,507	-$ 89,228			

Real Value of Dr. Spendthrift's Debt in 2023 Dollars (Graph 3)

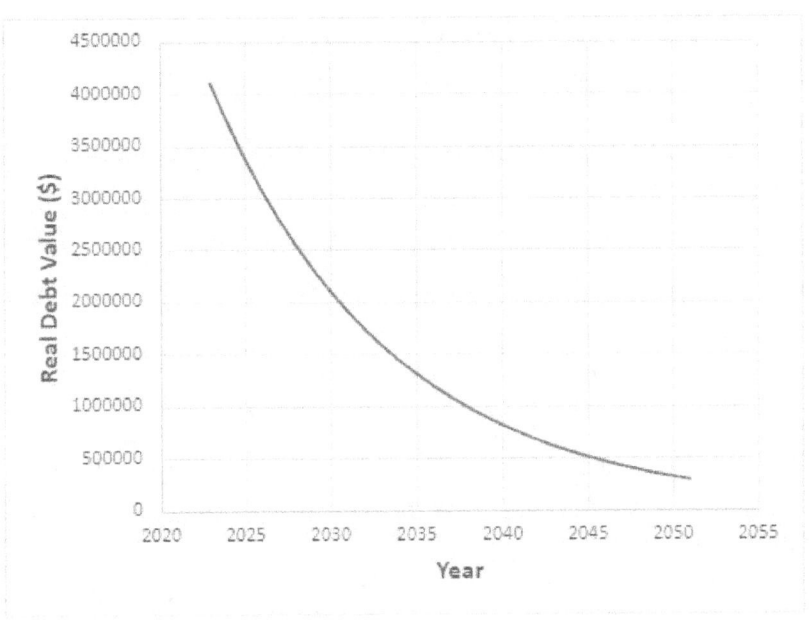

Don't get confused

This is where a lot of people get confused. They do not understand how debt can get "cheaper." But let's look at this concept from the perspective of how much time and effort it would take for Dr. Spendthrift to pay off his $4.1 million debt.

Dr. Spendthrift makes $250/hour in 2023. At that wage, he would have to work 16,400 hours to entirely pay off his $4.1 million mortgage. That is a Herculean task, but luckily for Dr. Spendthrift, he only needs to pay the interest expense on his debt – $287,000 a year or $23,917 a month – to keep the debt collectors away.

Dr. Spendthrift must work 1,148 hours a year or 96 hours a month to cover his interest expense. That is 57% of his income just to pay the interest on his debt. Since Dr. Spendthrift has many more expenses than just interest on his debt, we understand why he can't sleep at night. Fortunately for Dr. Spendthrift, inflation lends a helping hand.

Recall that both Dr. Frugal and Dr. Spendthrift's employment contract stipulates that they get a cost-of-living adjustment equal to rate of inflation every year. Dr. Spendthrift starts out in 2023 making $250/hour. After a year of 10% inflation, his wage rises to $275/hour and the year after that to $302.50/hour. By 2031 his hourly wage had more than doubled to $536/hour. Finally, after 30 years of 10% inflation his hourly wage is $4,362.

This is where the magic happens.

Remember, Dr. Spendthrift's interest rate is fixed. So, after 30 years his annual interest expense is still $287,000 but inflation has increased his hourly wage from $250 to $4,362. Instead of having to work 1,148 hours a year to pay his interest expense, now he only has to work 66 hours.

Inflation has been his friend. It has decreased, by 94%, the effort and time that Dr. Spendthrift must expend to carry his debt. It has made his debt "cheaper" by significantly reducing the workload needed to service it. Over time, inflation made Dr. Spendthrift's life much easier.

But inflation did not just make the annual cost of servicing Dr. Spendthrift's debt cheaper. It also made his total debt of $4.1 million cheaper. His debt started out in 2023 costing him 16,400 hours of work, but after 30 years of 10% inflation, it only cost him 940 hours of work. Priced in dollars, his debt and interest expense stayed the same for three decades. But priced in hours worked, his debt and interest expense got significantly cheaper. His total assets – his homes, etc. – increased their value at the same rate of inflation and after 30 years were still worth 16,400 work hours. Dr. Spendthrift could sell one of his vacation properties and pay off all of his debt with well over $13 million to spare.

This is such an important point that I will repeat it. Dr. Spendthrift's spectacular increase in net worth after 30 years was not a result of the real appreciation of his assets. His assets merely kept pace with inflation. Their value had the same purchasing power at the start of the 30-year period as at the end.

Paradoxically, the key to his wealth creation was his debt. Nominally, his debt remained the same but over time it decreased in real value. To put it another way, the total amount of his debt stayed the same – $4.1 million – but it could be paid off with increasingly devalued dollars. The purchasing power required to pay off his debt dramatically decreased because of inflation.

Inflation ate away at his debt at a rate of 10% a year. And when it comes to your net worth, decreasing your liabilities is just as important as increasing your assets. And, when taxes are considered, decreasing your liabilities is even more valuable than increasing your assets. You have to pay taxes when you realize the gains on your assets, but declines in your liabilities are tax free. More on that later when we discuss taxes.

Ironically, Dr. Spendthrift never realized why his wealth dramatically increased. He just thought he made great investments in real estate. But his real estate never appreciated in real terms. It was the depreciation of his debt, in real terms, that created his windfall. His fixed-rate debt was the secret to his success. His fixed-rate mortgage and student loans were his inflation hedge.

Taxes on Phantom Gains

It doesn't seem fair that big-spending Dr. Spendthrift overtook prudent Dr. Frugal in wealth. Dr. Frugal did OK. His net worth in real terms decreased slightly, but he basically kept up with inflation. It could have been a lot worse. Still, because he had no fixed-rate debt that could be devalued by inflation, Dr. Frugal missed out on the big windfalls enjoyed by debt-laden Dr.

Spendthrift. Sadly, when taxes are taken into consideration it gets even worse for Dr. Frugal.

Dr. Frugal's assets grew tax free for 30 years, which is great. His buy-and-hold strategy allowed his assets to keep pace with inflation without constantly being whittled away by taxes. But when Dr. Frugal retired in 2053, he needed to liquidate his traditional IRA so that he could pay his living expenses.

For simplicity's sake, we will assume that his IRA's starting value was $2 million (cost basis), and that he sold his entire portfolio all at once. Dr. Frugal bought the stocks in his portfolio for $2 million and sold them in 2053 for $34,898,804 -- a net gain of $32,898,804. It's an impressive amount at first glance, but remember, Dr. Frugal's stock portfolio only kept up with inflation. He had no real gains.

His stock portfolio in 2053 had the same purchasing power it had in 2023. But the government didn't see it like that. To the government, Dr. Frugal made a healthy profit of nearly $33 million dollars. And guess what? The taxman wanted his cut.

Since Dr. Frugal and his wife were now empty nesters and wanted to downsize their living arrangements, they sell their home and buy a nice little condo close to their children. The sale nets them $15,949,402 in capital gains.

In total, Dr. Frugal now has $48,848,206 in capital gains from the liquidation of his IRA and sale of his home. You can imagine the IRS agents salivating in the wings.

Dr. Frugal is in the highest tax bracket of 20% for long-term capital gains, which is much better than his 37% ordinary income tax rate. But on top of the 20% capital gains tax, he owes an additional 3.8% for the Medicare surtax. All in, he owes the U.S. Treasury 23.8% of his total capital gains from his stock market liquidation and the sale of his house.

On April 15, Dr. Frugal's CPA hands him a capital gains tax

bill of $11,625,873. After paying the taxes, Dr. Frugal's net worth is reduced to $40,822,633. The taxes decreased Dr. Frugal's net worth by 22.2%.

The worst part about this scenario is that after 30 years Dr. Frugal didn't actually make any real gains. He only had phantom gains created by inflation. His assets had the same purchasing power in 2023 as they did in 2053. Unfairly, the IRS doesn't take inflation into account when determining our tax liability. At least Dr. Frugal's assets kept up with inflation, but it could just have easily underperformed inflation. In that scenario, Dr. Frugal might have had to pay taxes on phantom gains but would actually have suffered real losses.

Dr. Frugal did everything right. He did everything the financial gurus and talking heads told him to do. He lived within his means. He paid down his debts. And he saved for retirement. But he couldn't seem to get any traction. He was slipping farther and farther behind. After adjusting for inflation, Dr. Frugal's after-tax net worth in 2053 is $2,339,486 (in 2023 dollars). Which is $760,514 less than the $3,100,000 he started with 30 years earlier.

On the other hand, our friend Dr. Spendthrift did not have to pay any taxes on his windfall. If you recall, he had three 30-year interest-only mortgages with balloon payments due at the end. At the end of the 30 years, Dr. Spendthrift did a cash-out refinancing on his properties.

With this financing he was able to make the total balloon payments of $4 million on all of his three properties and secure traditional 30-year fixed-interest rate mortgages on each of them. After paying off his previous mortgages and leaving 20% equity in his properties he was able to cash out $51,838,086 ($2,970,766 in 2023 dollars). The government does not see that as income or capital gains. They, correctly, see it as debt and therefore no taxes are due. We will talk about Cash-out Refinancing later.

But wait, it gets better for Dr. Spendthrift. Not only did he not have to pay taxes on his windfall, he can continue to deduct the interest from his primary residence's new mortgage, and if he decides to rent out his two vacation properties, he can tax deduct their mortgage interest from their rental income.

Just when you think it can't get any better for Dr. Spendthrift, it does. Remember his silver coin collection? It increased in price from $100,000 in 2023 to $1,744,940 in 2053. In 2023, both his coin collection and his student loans were $100,000. However, his coin collection kept up with inflation, and in 2053 it was worth $1,744,940. But his student loan was fixed and in 2053 it was still only $100,000.

Dr. Spendthrift sold a small portion of his coin collection for $100,000 and used the proceeds to pay off his student loan debt. Technically, the profit from the sale is a taxable capital gain, but it didn't occur to Dr. Spendthrift to report it to the IRS and no taxes were paid on the transaction.

Recall that Dr. Frugal saved in dollars. The balance of his savings account started out at $100,000 in 2023 and only increased $300 to $100,300 by 2053. Dr. Spendthrift saved silver coins, which unlike Dr. Frugal's decaying dollars maintained their purchasing power.

So who gets to retire?
Dr. Frugal, now 65, is confronted with the real possibility of living another 25 or 30 years. He was proud of the gains in his investments, but he just does not feel as secure as he expected. God knows, he is doing much better than most people in the country. But the cost of living in 2053 is sky high.

His newly purchased downsized condo will cost nearly $20 million and the property taxes are outrageous. Dr. Frugal decides that he will continue to work full time for another five years. He hopes by then he will have saved enough to retire comfortably and worry free.

Meanwhile, Dr. Spendthrift, also 65, is flush with cash from his recent cash-out refinancing. He has been researching "around the world" cruises. Many of his big-spending friends fell on hard times, so this time it will just be him and his wife. With no income coming in from employment, he figures he will do short-term rentals with his vacation homes to at least pay the bills. One thing he definitely won't be doing is going back to work at the hospital. He has hung up his stethoscope for good.

Dr. Spendthrift's retirement and continued extravagant lifestyle surprises Dr. Frugal. He assumes that Dr. Spendthrift or his wife inherited a ton of money. He shrugs his shoulders and thinks, "Some guys have all the luck."

Dr. Spendthrift did get lucky. He walked backwards into a windfall all because inflation devalued the real value of his debt. He did not plan for it or really understand it when it happened. This is true for millions of Americans who had a similar lucky windfall from the 1970s to the present as real estate values soared but their home mortgages were locked in at a fixed rate.

They say "Luck favors the prepared mind." And now that you know how inflation can work to your benefit, you can learn how to make your own luck — and wealth.

Chapter 4

Inflation Proofing Your Wealth is Easy

Self-defense is not only our right; it is our duty.
–Ronald Reagan

Most people have neither the financial knowledge or the wherewithal to protect their wealth from inflation. That's why most people will be crushed by the destructive inflationary wave that has already arrived. But I'm here to tell you there are some simple strategies you can learn to inflation-proof your wealth. They are easy, expense-free and require only minimal active participation. With a little forethought and planning, they will save you – and your wealth – from the worst that inflation will bring.

Don't Save in Dollars
The first step in inflation proofing your wealth is to not be a creditor. Don't be a person to whom money is owed directly or indirectly. This means not saving or lending in dollars. Dr. Frugal's and Dr. Spendthrift's financial stories demonstrate how inflation transfers wealth from creditors to debtors – from the people who already have money to lend to the people who borrow it.

When Dr. Frugal deposited $100,000 into a savings account, earning 0.01% interest, the bank turned right around and lent out his $100,000 to people like Dr. Spendthrift in the form of mortgages. That essentially made Dr. Frugal a creditor – a creditor who was getting a very lousy rate of return on his money.

When inflation rose to 10%, the real interest rate on Dr. Frugal's savings account at the bank became a negative 9.99%. This means the purchasing power of his $100,000 dropped virtually $9,000 in just one year. Simultaneously, the real value of Dr. Spendthrift's debt shrunk by 9.1% annually.

After 20 years of 10% annual inflation, we saw how Dr. Frugal's savings account had lost 94% of its real purchasing power while the value of Dr. Spendthrift's debt decreased by 94%. Through inflation, which steadily ate away at the value of every dollar, the government confiscated 94% of Dr. Frugal's savings account and transferred it to itself and debtors like Dr. Spendthrift.

Inflation transferred the purchasing power of diligent savers like Dr. Frugal to free-spending debtors like Dr. Spendthrift. Ironically, Dr. Frugal still had to pay taxes on the minuscule interest he received from his original $100,000 savings account at the bank even though its purchasing power was nearly obliterated by three decades of inflation.

Dr. Frugal, sorry to say, was a relic of a bygone era. He thought he was being responsible by saving and not borrowing, but really he was just being a sucker. In real terms, he was paying debtors to borrow his money.

Today it does not pay to put your dollars in a bank, but it wasn't always like that. Our great-grandparents and grandparents had savings accounts, certificates of deposits and U.S. Savings Bonds because it made sense to save cash back then. Back then, the interest rate you got from your savings in a bank or a CD was significantly higher than the annual rate of inflation. Believe it or not, people actually used to be able to retire on the interest income they got from their savings accounts or government bonds.

These days hardly anyone saves any significant amount of their wealth in cash. Sure, they might briefly park dollars in savings and checking accounts while they're in-between investments or waiting to make a large purchase.

But people understand, if only subconsciously, that they're losing money by saving their cash. They can see their savings standing still and earning near-zero interest while the price of everything else skyrockets. They know they cannot expect to keep up, much less get ahead, with savings alone.

Out of necessity yesterday's confident savers have become today's reluctant investors. Knowing that the days of simply stashing their cash in a savings account are over, these ex-savers must now make increasingly risky investments in the quest for what passes today as a decent yield.

Where our great grandparents used to reliably make a 5% to 7% real return in nearly riskless investments like savings accounts or certificates of deposits, investors today speculate on unprofitable companies with sky-high valuations. Or they rely on unproven technologies like cryptocurrency in the hope of eking out a positive yield that will somehow magically fund their retirement.

Holding your dollars in cash outside of the financial system is even worse than putting it in a bank. At least with a savings account you might make a couple bucks a month in interest. Idle cash simply decays – both figuratively and literally. Inflation destroys its value and time destroys its physical properties; it's just paper after all.

Graph 2 from Chapter 3 shows the value of $100 in cash compared to the value of an ounce of silver priced in terms of each other over time. Visually, the trend is strikingly obvious. Priced in dollars, the price of silver grows exponentially while the value of the dollar plummets at the same rate.

It is not that silver's value necessarily increases over time, it is that the value of the dollar needed to buy an ounce of silver decreases with near certainty. Knowing this, would you rather store your wealth in silver bullion or $100 bills?

The larger point here is that you should never save in large amounts of dollars, whether you put them in a bank account or you hide the cash under your mattress. You should store your wealth in an asset whose value will not be eroded by inflation. That could be real estate, stocks or precious metals.

Personally, I keep enough dollars in my checking to cover my monthly expenses and transfer the rest to my brokerage account. Whatever asset you choose to store your wealth in, make sure it keeps up with inflation and keep a portion of your wealth in something like gold or silver coins that can be easily converted into currency. In later chapters, we will delve deeper into safe strategies for saving in high inflation environments.

Don't Lend in Dollars, either

One of the easiest things you can do to mitigate the damage of inflation is to avoid loaning your dollars at a fixed rate for a long period of time. Recall that Dr. Spendthrift went from broke to multimillionaire after two decades simply by paying only the interest on his large loans.

He produced nothing of value for 30 years, so where did all that newly acquired wealth of his come from? Answer: It was transferred to him from the bank that held his mortgages and, in effect, it came from the bank's depositors.

Consider another hypothetical example of Mr. John Smith, a successful business owner with a ne'er-do-well son-in-law, Jimmy, who's married to Mr. Smith's daughter. Jimmy wants to buy a home for his beautiful new bride, but unfortunately does not have the necessary credit or collateral to obtain a mortgage.

Jimmy approaches Mr. Smith with an investment opportunity. He proposes that Mr. Smith lends him $300,000 to buy a modest home for him and Mr. Smith's daughter to live. It will be an interest-only 5-year loan at a rate of 5% with the principal due at the end of the term.

Mr. Smith knows that inflation is only 2% – the Federal Reserve's target inflation rate. He calculates the real interest rate, and is delighted that it is positive at 3% (5% - 2%). Mr. Smith considers the investment and determines that if everything works out he will make $75,000 in interest and his daughter will have a nice home.

The worst that can happen is Jimmy defaults and Mr. Smith can foreclose on a home that most likely has appreciated while keeping up all interest payments until the point of foreclosure.

Over the course of the first year, Jimmy makes his payments in full and on time. Inflation remains at 2% and everything looks great. Then at about the one-year mark inflation ticks up to 3%.

Now Mr. Smith's real interest rate is 2% (5% - 3%). It is still positive, but it is unlikely that he would have originally made the loan if the real interest rate was just 2%. While it is true that the loan is not as profitable now that inflation is higher, Jimmy is still making timely payments, so Mr. Smith still has a real positive return. He is making money.

Right around year two, however, inflation ticks up to 5%. Now Mr. Smith's real interest rate is 0% (5% - 5%). Now he is essentially loaning his money out for free. That is not entirely accurate because the government will continue to tax his interest income. So Mr. Smith will actually be losing money after taxes. Still, it's not a complete disaster. Jimmy is still making interest payments and Mr. Smith fully expects to be repaid his entire principal.

Year three rolls around and Jimmy and Mr. Smith's daughter

divorce. Jimmy keeps the house. Inflation is really heating up. It is now 10% annually. Mr. Smith's real interest rate is now minus 5% (5% -10% = -5%). Ironically, Mr. Smith is now paying Jimmy 5% annually in purchasing power to borrow his money. Of course, the IRS still expects Mr. Smith to pay taxes on his interest income.

The home Jimmy is living in has increased significantly in value, and Mr. Smith finds himself actively hoping Jimmy defaults, so that he can foreclose. No such luck. Jimmy continues to make his monthly payments in full and on time.

Year four gets even worse as inflation ramps up even higher to 12%. The good news for Mr. Smith is that Jimmy never missed a payment. The bad news for Mr. Smith is Jimmy never missed a payment and Mr. Smith was never able to foreclose. At the end of the 5-year term, Jimmy pays the last interest payment along with the principal of $300,000. Jimmy's home is now worth almost twice its purchase price.

Mr. Smith was paid every dime he was owed, but he could not help but feel that he got the short end of the stick. Jimmy returned Mr. Smith's principal nominally intact, albeit with its original purchasing power drastically reduced by inflation. Mr. Smith's lost purchasing power was transferred to Jimmy. Adding insult to injury, the IRS taxed Mr. Smith on all the interest income he received while Jimmy not only avoided paying taxes on his windfall, he tax-deducted the interest payments.

You are probably thinking, "I'm not a bank or hard money lender. I don't lend people money. The above example does not apply to me."

Are you sure about that? Do you have a bank account? Certificate of Deposits (CDs)? Bonds? Then I have news for you. You lend people money. You are a creditor.

You probably thought that when you deposit funds into a savings or checking account you became a customer of the bank. In reality, you became a creditor to the bank. This makes sense when you think about it. You deposit funds into a bank account and the bank lends out your funds to homebuyers, small businesses, large corporations and even the U.S. government. The bank is merely a middleman deploying your funds to borrowers. You are the real creditor.

This is why Dr. Frugal and other savers get killed in periods of high inflation. They essentially lend out their money at a negative real interest rate. Lending at a negative interest rate means you are paying the borrower in purchasing power to borrow your money.

When you deposit your money into a bank, that is exactly what you are doing. You are loaning your money at a measly rate of 0.01% or less while the official target rate of inflation is around 2 percent. That means your real interest rate is around minus 1.99%. Inflation of 2%, by the way, is the best-case scenario. Actual inflation can be much higher than the official target rate.

Saving money in a bank is a loser's game. I defy you to find an accredited FDIC-insured bank in the United States that currently gives you a higher rate of interest on your savings than even the officially stated rate of inflation. To my knowledge, every savings account in the United States is currently earning a negative real interest rate.

Bonds and Certificates of Deposits (CDs) are even worse. Sure, the interest rate on them is higher than a savings account, but they lock-in your dollars for months and sometimes years at a time. At least with a savings account, you can withdraw your dollars on demand.

But what happens if your money is in bonds or CDs and there is a spike in inflation? Your real interest rate will just turn even more negative and your dollars are locked in. You could sell your bonds or CDs but it'd be at a huge loss. Either way, you are going to lose wealth and purchasing power.

As of mid-November 2022, the current yield on a 30-year Treasury Bond was just 3.98% while the inflation rate, measured by the CPI, was 7.1%. If you bought a 30-year Treasury bond in November 2022 your real interest rate would be negative 3.12% (3.98% minus 7.1%).

Even if you believe the CPI is an accurate measure of inflation, which I don't (I think it significantly understates inflation), you are still earning a negative real interest rate. Can you imagine losing purchasing power year after year for 30 years? That's exactly what will happen if you buy bonds that yield less than the rate of inflation and hold them to maturity.

U.S. Treasuries bonds are considered "riskless" assets, but that's only because the U.S. Treasury can and will print money to pay off the debt. Of course, this means you will be paid in future dollars that will have less purchasing power.

The traditional financial advice of splitting your investment portfolio into 60% equities and 40% bonds is no longer prudent. In fact, it will probably lead to a significantly delayed retirement -- if you get to have one at all. If you only take one thing away from this book, let it be this: Do not be a long-term holder of bonds.

One possible exception are TIPS – Treasury Inflation Protected Securities. They are U.S. Treasury Bonds where the principal of the bond is indexed to inflation as measured by the CPI. The inflation adjustment is made semi-annually.

The biggest problem with TIPS is that they are indexed to the CPI, which was specifically designed by the government to understate inflation. Also, any adjustment upward of your principal is considered taxable income even though you have not yet received any actual dollars. Furthermore, TIPS start out with even lower initial interest rates than other U.S. Treasuries. Nevertheless, if I had to invest in U.S. Treasuries, I would invest in TIPS.

You are probably wondering, "If bonds are such a bad investment, why do so many Wall Street hedge funds and elite investment banks invest in bonds?"

It is true that some people make enormous profits investing with bonds. But that's from trading bonds, not holding the bonds long term and getting the interest payments. These big traders know the real yield for these bonds is negative, but they are speculating that they can harvest a capital gain by timing the volatility of the bond.

An example of this is the Argentinian century bond – a 100-year bond issued in 2017 by the Argentinian government with a coupon of 7.125%, nearly three times higher than what a U.S. treasury bond was paying. The demand for this bond was strong and the Argentinean government sold nearly $3 billion worth.

This is surprising considering Argentina is a serial defaulter. I doubt you could go back in history and find a 20-year period where the Argentinian government has not defaulted, much less a century. Nevertheless, bond investors snapped them up and, like clockwork, the Argentinians defaulted just 3 years into the 100-year maturity. Now some people made out in this transaction. The Argentinian government made $3 billion and there were probably a few slick bond traders who made a couple hundred million dollars. But the long-term investor, he got wiped out.

If you're smart enough to trade bonds profitably, then, by all means, go with God. You have my blessing. As for me, I am not that smart. I will continue to avoid an asset class that is guaranteed to have a negative real return if it's held long term.

To sum up the follies of saving or lending in dollars, remember the realities. You and I cannot print money like the government. We have to work hard for our dollars, and it is impossible for us to obtain a real positive return from holding a 30-year U.S. Treasury Bond to maturity when it is only yielding 3% or a savings account with a 0.01% APR. Preserve your net worth by not saving or lending in dollars.

Do Not Lend to Family and Friends

Hopefully, by now you are starting to detect a trend. In the setting of high inflation, lending money to people or places is the fastest way to decrease your future purchasing power. That being said, there may be instances when we feel compelled or pressured to loan money to a friend or family member.

Periods of high inflation are often fraught with economic turmoil, and a lot of people will find themselves ill-prepared and in bad financial situations. And since you are reading this book, we can assume that your economic situation is passably sound and probably even prosperous. There is a very good chance that you're not-so-fortunate friends and family will ask you for a loan. When this happens, channel your inner Nancy Reagan and just say "No."

Lending to friends and family is a money losing endeavor even in the best of economic times. The problem, of course, is that it is difficult to charge close relations a fair interest rate.

Friends and family usually don't want to pay *any* interest much less a rate that reflects inflation and the risk of non-payment. Even if they manage to pay the loan back to you, in a period of high inflation it will be worth a fraction of its original value.

My personal history of loaning cash to friends is that I either lost the cash or I lost the friend, and sometimes I lost both. If you do decide to make a loan to a friend or family member, then consider it a gift from the start. If you get paid back, it will be a welcome surprise. If you don't get paid back, you helped a friend in need.

Do Not Payoff Fixed Low-interest Debt Early

If you have any fixed low-interest debt like a home mortgage, student loans or car debt, then never pay them off early. I know this is counter-intuitive to what we have always been taught and contrary to what many popular financial advisors and pundits like Dave Ramsey advocate.

We have been taught to avoid debt and if we get in debt then we should work to pay it down as quickly as possible. This is certainly true for variable and high-interest debt like credit cards or so-called payday loans. But for a fixed low-interest long-term loan, in a high inflation environment it is always in your best interest to pay the monthly minimum payments and no more.

For example, two years ago I got a five-year loan for my new car at a 2.9% interest rate. That was a great rate on a loan for what was once considered a depreciating asset. But now the prices of new and used cars have increased so dramatically that the dealership is offering to buy back that same car from me for $2,500 more than I paid for it. Essentially, I would get paid $2,500 for putting 25,000 miles on my car.

I did not accept the offer. If I had several cars laying around my garage, I might have. But I need a car. If I sold my only one back to the dealership, my $2,500 profit would not go very far toward the purchase of a new car at today's much higher prices.

Remember, inflation is a debtor's best friend because it eats away at the value of your debt. Recall the example of Dr. Spendthrift. He only made monthly minimum payments while inflation worked night and day to decay the value of his debt. After 20 years, he went from having 0% equity in his house to a 94% equity position without ever once paying a dollar of the principal.

Avoid Annuities

An annuity is a contract with a financial company, often an insurance company, where you give them a lump sum of your money and they give you a fixed-interest payment over a set amount of time or even for life.

An annuity behaves essentially like a bond. Typically, you will receive a lower interest rate than from a bond. It's a tiny real rate of return if you believe the government's official inflation rate, but if high inflation or, God forbid, hyperinflation hits, you're wiped out. The purchasing power of your fixed interest payments gets decimated, and you're stuck with an illiquid financial instrument that you will only be able to exit by taking a huge loss.

Financial advisors love annuities because of the huge commissions they get selling them. Admittedly, there are many different types of annuities, including some that are indexed to the stock market and even the CPI. Some insurance companies even offer inflation riders. But in a period of high inflation, you never want to be the guy that is getting paid back piecemeal after initially lending a big pile of dollars. You want to be on the other side of this trade. In short, you want to be the borrower, not the lender.

Consider Early Payout of Fixed Income

If you are working and your wages don't keep up with inflation, you can always switch jobs. Unfortunately, if you must depend on fixed income payments from a pension, Social Security, annuities, insurance products, lawsuit settlement payouts, alimony/child support, lottery winnings, etc., keeping up with high inflation will be challenging.

Social Security and many private pensions have cost of living adjustments (COLA). But these COLAs are almost exclusively indexed to the CPI which, as stated before, is intentionally designed to understate true inflation. This understatement widens as the inflation rate gets higher.

It is unlikely that pension or Social Security administrators would voluntarily raise their cost-of-living adjustments beyond what is required by law or contract. As I see it, there are really only two options you have to defend your fixed income payments from inflation and, I'm sorry to say, neither will make you whole with regard to the purchasing power you were expecting.

The first option is obvious and it's the same with all forms of income. After meeting your immediate needs, convert any excess income into real assets. The problem is that each successive fixed income payment you receive has continuously decaying purchasing power.

In periods of high inflation, your fixed income payment will not even cover your living expenses much less your investment objectives. Once your fixed income fails to cover your monthly bills, it is time to go back to work. As economist Peter Schiff has noted, retirement, like having a stay-at-home wife, will be reserved only for the wealthy.

The second way to defend your fixed income payments from inflation, if available, is to obtain an upfront lump-sum pay out. There will likely be tax penalties and possibly early withdrawal penalties associated with it, but to keep it simple let's assume no penalties. Even without taking into consideration any penalties, the early lump sum payment will be considerably less than the nominal value of your annuity or pension income stream.

To understand why this is, we must first understand the concept of present value. The present value (PV) of a sum or income stream of dollars is the amount that would have to be invested now at a particular interest rate to obtain the same sum in the future. Therefore, the administrator of the annuity or pension will not pay you the full amount of the annuity or pension. They will pay you a lump sum that will achieve the full amount of the annuity or pension after the specified time period at the assumed interest rate.

For example, let's say you have an annuity that pays you $5,000 monthly for the next 10 years. The total sum of all payments would be $600,000 ($5,000 x 12 x 10 = $600,000). However, assuming an interest rate of 2.5%, then the annuity's present value is $530,392. This is because if you had $530,392 and used it to buy a bond at a 2.5% annual interest rate you would earn $69,608 in interest after 10 years. If we assume an interest rate of 5%, the present value is $471,407; at a 7.5% interest rate, then the present value is $421,224.

These calculations can get pretty complicated, but the most important thing to remember is the higher the assumed interest rate is, the lower the present value of the annuity. Another point that needs to be understood is that the higher the inflation rate, the higher the interest rate.

To obtain a real positive return, lenders and investors require a higher interest or rate of return than the rate of inflation. So, all else being equal, the higher inflation rate, the higher the interest rate, and the lower the present value.

That is really all you have to know about present value and it is worth repeating: The higher the inflation rate, the lower the present value of an income stream from an annuity, pension or anything that promises to pay you in the future.

OK, so how do we use this information to our advantage?

Simple. If the organization that pays your annuity or pension expects low inflation, but instead we get high inflation, then they will overvalue the present value of the annuity/pension. In other words, you could potentially get an early lump sum payment that is higher than its true present value.

Let's go back to our earlier example: You have an annuity that pays you $5,000 monthly for the next 10 years. The annuity's economists expect a period of relatively lower inflation for the next decade and predict an interest rate of 2.5%. You, on the other hand, expect high inflation and predict an interest rate of 7.5%.

You ask the annuity administrator for an early withdrawal. Assuming an interest rate of 2.5%, he does the calculations and offers you a lump sum payment of $530,392. You also run the numbers, but assume an interest rate of 7.5%. You calculate the fair present value of your annuity to be $421,224. Since the annuity administrator is offering you a lump sum payment that is $109,168 more than what you think it is worth, you take the deal ($530,392 − $421,224 = $109,168).

The good news is that you are right. Over the subsequent 10 years, inflation is high and you were able to buy 10-year U.S. Treasury bonds yielding 7.5% with your $421,224 lump sum. After 10 years your lump sum payment grows to $1,093,155, which is $493,155 more than the total $600,000 you would have received if you had just continued to receive the $5,000 monthly payments for 10 years.

The bad news is that since inflation was so high, your real return is most certainly negative. But on the bright side, it is still larger than if you had just continued to take the monthly fixed payments.

Draw Your Social Security at Age 62

You can start drawing your Social Security as early as age 62, which is 5 years earlier than the official retirement age of 67 (yes, they increased it to 67 if you were born in 1960 or after). The catch is that if you take your Social Security benefit early it reduces the amount you receive by a certain percentage for each month you retire early.

If you retire 5 years (or 60 months) early, then they reduce your monthly payments by 30%. A 30% reduction in your monthly payment is a big hit to take, but remember you will be getting 60 monthly payments that you wouldn't have otherwise gotten.

Now obviously if you knew exactly when you were going to die it would be much easier to calculate the optimal scenario. If you are going to die at age 63, start taking the payments as early as possible so at least you get something. If you are going to live to 120, then early retirement probably isn't a priority.

Calculating the optimal time to start drawing your Social Security is very person-specific because you must consider your birth year, payroll contributions, personal tax rate, marital status and expected life expectancy.

However, assuming a reasonable return on investment (ROI), and if you plan on investing all of your early payments, then withdrawing your Social Security benefits early nearly always outperforms withdrawing them later. High inflation tips the balance even more to withdrawing early. And the higher the inflation rate is, the more withdrawing early outperforms drawing later.

If you expect future high inflation or very high inflation, which I do, then it is imperative to withdraw your Social Security early. While it is true that Social Security is indexed to the CPI, the CPI was explicitly adjusted to reduce the increasing cost of Social Security and other entitlements.

Of course, the benefit of getting your Social Security early is predicated on investing the withdrawn money. If your money is immediately spent, then the benefit of early withdrawal diminishes and may disappear altogether. However, if the inflation rate is very high, it doesn't matter whether you invest or spend your Social Security check. It's always better to withdraw your benefits early.

Summary

The easiest and cheapest way to inflation proof your wealth is to not be a creditor or some variation of the theme. This means not lending your dollars to:

    ☐   Banks – i.e., via savings accounts, certificates of deposits (CDs)

    ☐   Governments – U.S. Treasuries, municipal bonds, etc.

    ☐   Corporations – corporate bonds

    ☐   Annuities – a fancy type of bond

Understand that this advice is completely contrary to mainstream financial dogma.

FDIC-insured savings accounts, CDs and government bonds are considered the safest of all assets. In fact, U.S. Treasuries are so safe they are considered riskless. It is true that you will almost certainly get all of your principal returned to you, but it will just have much less purchasing power than when you lent it.

Remember that the real interest rate is the key determinant of whether or not you are losing purchasing power, and the real interest rate is calculated by subtracting the inflation rate from the interest rate you are receiving. And most of all, remember that if the real interest rate is negative, you are losing purchasing power and should not make that investment.

Chapter 5

What Makes a Good Inflation Hedge?

Invest in Inflation. It is the only thing that is going up.
–Will Rogers

It should be obvious by now that high inflation steadily and mercilessly erodes the purchasing power of your cash and makes lending and saving in dollars a losing proposition. That means we must find alternative means of preserving our wealth. This is called "hedging against inflation" – i.e., converting our dollars into real assets that will, at a minimum, preserve our wealth during periods of inflation.

Unfortunately, most of the things we consider to be assets, like cars and electronics, depreciate over time just like our dollars. So, choosing the right asset is critical to safely storing our wealth. This raises the question: What properties should an inflation hedge possess?

The perfect inflation hedge has the following attributes:

- ☐ Store of value
- ☐ Income producing
- ☐ Liquidity/Portability
- ☐ Durability
- ☐ Favorable tax and political treatment

Many inflation hedges have some but not all of these properties. We will focus on equities (stocks, ETFs, mutual funds, etc.), real estate, precious metals and commodities since they are the most common hedges against inflation. I will also comment on the fitness of cryptocurrencies as an inflation hedge, since they have become much more prominent, especially among younger investors.

Store of Value

When an asset maintains its value in good and bad times and everything in between, it is said to be a store of value. Maintaining its value is by far the most important attribute to consider when choosing an asset to store your wealth.

During high inflation just about everything goes up in price. The trick is to own an asset whose value will increase at least as much as inflation. Equities, real estate and precious metals nearly always increase in price during times of inflation. Each of those asset classes will always outperform cash during high inflation, but which one will perform the best?

How well an asset does during bouts of high inflation depends on a number of larger variables like the economic and political landscape, war and peace, etc. For example, during the infamous hyperinflation in the Weimar Republic in the early 1920s, when the value of the German mark was reduced to virtually zero, the price of gold in Germany increased nearly twice as fast as the rate of inflation.

Yet during the high inflation of the 1940s in the United States, the price of gold in our country barely budged. Why? Because in 1933 President Franklin D. Roosevelt had issued an executive order that set the price of gold at $20.67 per ounce and outlawed gold ownership by private U.S. citizens.

Until the current spike in inflation, the last time the United States experienced significant inflation was in the 1970s. In the mid-1960s, as the federal government was spending heavily on the nuclear arms race with the Soviet Union and becoming more deeply mired in the costly war in Vietnam, and LBJ's expensive "Great Society" social programs began to ramp up.

The federal "War on Poverty" plus the new entitlement of Medicare cost billions. And who could forget the "Space Race"? To pay for all this welfare and warfare at home and abroad in the '70s, the government in Washington was forced to print more money – i.e., devalue the U.S. dollar and spike inflation.

Foreign governments held, and still do, a lot of U.S. dollars as reserves in their own central banks. It was hard not to notice the unprecedented level of U.S. government spending, and they determined, correctly, that the U.S. increase of the supply of gold was not matching the increasing supply of dollars. This meant that U.S. was devaluing the dollar – including the dollars foreign governments held in reserve.

At this time, the U.S. was still on a gold standard. That meant that a foreign central bank could take their U.S. dollar reserves to the "gold window" at the Federal Reserve and exchange $35 for one ounce of gold, the official price of gold at the time. And they did ... en masse, creating a "run on the gold." Foreign central banks began exchanging U.S. dollars for cold hard gold. U.S. gold reserves dropped from 20,000 tons in the early 1950s to 8,500 tons in 1971. Currently, the United States has 8,133 tons of gold.

The United States faced a choice: 1. They could do nothing and have all of the U.S. gold reserves sucked out of the country. 2. They could revalue the gold closer to its market price, which was the same as devaluing the dollar. 3. They could stop printing dollars and dramatically scale back on welfare and warfare spending. 4. They could default on our foreign creditors by closing the gold window and ending the exchange of dollars for gold. (In 1933, President Roosevelt closed the gold window, the 1944 Bretton Woods Agreement of 1944 opened the gold window to foreign central banks.)

In 1971 the decision was never really in doubt. President Nixon could not allow all of the country's gold to be "withdrawn" from the country. Even today, a nation cannot have the global reserve currency without having significant gold reserves. Nixon also couldn't revalue the price of gold because it would be rightly perceived for what it was ... a devaluation of the dollar. Another big no-no for a reserve currency. Cutting government spending on social programs like Medicare and social security is not politically viable.

Predictably, on August 15, 1971, President Nixon "temporarily" closed the gold window, thereby closing the book on the last vestiges of the gold standard. Fifty-two years later, the gold window remains "temporarily" closed with the time and circumstances of its reopening to be determined.

To be sure, the closing of the gold window by President Nixon was a default by the U.S. federal government on anyone who held U.S. dollars. Since the dollar was the global reserve currency, that meant just about everyone. Instead of getting gold for their dollars, foreign central banks got ... well ... nothing.

Miraculously, however, all of our trading partners accepted this default despite the value of their dollar holdings being slashed. Perhaps, they realized that with the U.S. dollar no longer anchored to gold their currency was no longer anchored to gold vis-a-vis the dollar. They were now free to print a sufficient amount of their own currencies to support their own social programs and projects.

Of course, the closing of the gold window did come at a price for the holders of U.S. dollars. With the last tether between gold and the Yankee dollar cut, the government in Washington continued its profligate spending and the value of the dollar dropped at an ever-increasing rate. The double-digit inflation of the 1970s is the most recent bout of high inflation in the United States and it is instructive to see how our inflation hedges performed back then.

Table 6 shows the 1971 and 1981 CPI levels and the S&P 500 and gold prices at market close on Friday, August 13, 1971 compared to the same data ten years later on August 13, 1981. August 13, 1971 is significant because it was the last stock market close before Nixon shut the gold window on Sunday, August 15, 1971. The table also lists the median home prices in August 1971 and in August 1981. From this past data we can get an idea of how we might want to deploy our inflation hedges in the future.

Between 1971 and 1981, when the average annual rate of inflation was 8.42%, gold had the best performance of our inflation hedges, followed by single-family homes and stocks, respectively. Gold had a staggering real annual increase of 16.74%. Housing had a real average annual increase of 2.04%, which is not jaw dropping, but respectable.

The U.S. stock market, as measured by the S&P 500, did not keep up with inflation and showed a negative real average return. The average nominal annual return on the S&P 500 was 1.84%. But the annual inflation rate was 8.42%, which equates to a real annual return of - 6.58% (1.84% - 8.42% = - 6.58%).

That made it a terrible time to own equities. For example, if you bought an S&P 500 index fund in 1971, by 1981 it would have increased by 20%. But a decade of high inflation had cut the purchasing power of the dollar by 47.13% (See Table 6). That means that in 1981 the value of your original stock portfolio would have bought you only about half of what it did ten years earlier.

So, for example, assume that in 1971 your S&P 500 index fund was worth $100 and in 1971 a $100 bill could buy 100 doughnuts. In 1981 your S&P 500 index fund was worth $122 but in 1981 that sum could only buy 53 doughnuts (assuming that the price of doughnuts had increased at the rate of inflation).

Our other two hedges – housing and gold – fared much better in the 1970s.

In fact, in both cases the purchasing power of those assets increased. Housing appreciated by roughly 23%. For example, for every $100 worth of housing you owned in 1971, it would be worth an inflation-adjusted $122.55 in 1981. Gold performed even better. In 1971, $100 worth of gold could buy 100 doughnuts but in 1981 the same amount of gold could buy you 470 doughnuts.

It would be easy to assume from this that gold is the best inflation hedge, but we have to remember that it was only the best of the three assets we studied in this particular 10-year period. Gold hit a high of $843 January 21, 1980, but it was more than halved to $400 by December 31, 1981. It dropped another 36% over the next two decades to $255.95 on April 2, 2001.

The rise and fall of the price of gold speaks to the importance of diversification over the long term. It performed fantastically during the high inflation period of the 1970s but performed dismally over the relatively mild inflation of the 1980s and 1990s. Can you imagine being long gold in January of 1980 only to see the value of your holding reduced by 70% just 16 months later? And that's the nominal return. If you adjust for inflation, the pain was much worse.

Hopefully, you bought more gold as it fell all the way down to $256 an ounce, because starting in 2001 it had another huge leg up over inflation for the next 20 years. But even in those golden years as it steadily climbed to around its current price of about $2,000 an ounce, gold ranged from an intraday high of greater than $1,900 in 2011 to a low of $1,055 in 2015.

Change in Purchasing Power of Inflation Hedges, 1971-1981 (Table 6)

	1971	1981	%Total Increase	Avg. Annual Change	Real Avg. Annual Change	Real Change in Purchasing Power
CPI	40.5	90.9	124%	8.42%	-	-
S&P 500	102.09	122.55	20%	1.84%	-6.58%	-47%
Median Home Price	$25,300	$68,400	170%	10.46%	2.04%	22%
Gold 1 oz.	$43.48	$410.30	844%	25.16%	16.74%	370%

As we said, equities, as represented by the S&P 500, were a poor inflation hedge during the high inflation years of 1971 to 1981, losing 47% of their purchasing power. However, if we expand the time horizon an additional 40 years to 2021, we see that in the long run equities have performed exceptionally well.

In fact, stocks went from worst inflation hedge to the best. Between 1971 and 2021 the S&P 500 index's purchasing power increased by 653% (Table 7). In the same time period, gold's and housing's purchasing power increased by 558% and 146%, respectively.

Change in Purchasing Power of
Inflation Hedges, 1971-2021
(Table 7)

	1971	2021	% Increase	Avg. Annual Change	Real Avg. Annual Change	Change in Purchasing Power
CPI	40.5	271.4	570 %	570 %	-	-
S&P 500	95.69 *	4468 **	4569 %	4569 %	4.12 %	653 %
Median Home Sales Price	$25,300#	$404,300##	1498 %	1498 %	1.82 %	146 %
Gold 1 oz.	$43.27°	$1779 °°	4013 %	4013 %	3.84 %	558 %

*Close of the S&P 500 August 13, 1971. The last stock market close before President Nixon closed the gold window.
**Close of the S&P 500 August 13, 2021
Median Home Sales Price August, 1971
Median Home Sales Price August, 2021
°Gold Price at Market Close August 13, 1971. The last gold market close before Nixon closed the Gold Window.
°°Gold Price at Market Close August 12, 2021

All of our favorite hedges have performed well since Richard Nixon slammed the gold window shut in 1971 and opened the inflation door. They not only preserved our purchasing power, they increased it. If our wealth had been stored entirely in cash, instead of growing, our purchasing power would have been nearly wiped out.

Table 8 compares the purchasing power in 1971 of $100 in cash, S&P 500 stocks, housing and gold. In 1971 a $100 bill would have had the purchasing power of $100. But by 1981 its purchasing power had sunk to $44.56 and by 2021 it had crashed to $14.91. By contrast, $100 worth of housing, gold and S&P 500 stocks in 1971 would have had inflation-adjusted purchasing power in 2021 of $246.41, $658.01 and $752.85, respectively.

Purchasing Power of Cash and
Inflation Hedges, 1971-2021
(Table 8)

	Purchasing Power 1971	Purchasing Power 1981	Purchasing Power 2021
$100 Cash	$100	$44.56	$14.91
$100 of S&P 500 Index Fund	$100	$52.87	$752.85
$100 of Housing	$100	$122.38	$246.41
$100 of Gold	$100	$470.11	$658.01

If you take only one thing away from this book, let it be this:

DO NOT STORE YOUR WEALTH IN UNITED STATES FEDERAL RESERVE NOTES – aka, CASH.

Sure, keep some cash on hand for emergencies. Or if you are an investor, hold some dollars in reserve to buy a solid stock on the dip. But for God's and Murray Rothbard's sake, do not store a large portion of your wealth long-term in cash.

If you absolutely must store your wealth in cash, then do it in coins. Unlike paper, the base metals that make up pennies, nickels and quarters will keep up with inflation. It's illegal to melt or otherwise destroy U.S. currency, but the fact that coins have intrinsic value will preserve purchasing power.

Currently, a copper penny is worth several times its face value.

Depending on how wealthy you are, that's likely to require several self-storage units filled with tons of change. So you might want to consider some or all of our aforementioned inflation hedges.

Income Producing

Proponents of equities and real estate as investments will argue that their true appreciation in value is understated because it does not reflect their cash flow. Critics of gold, notably Warren Buffet, state the obvious that gold has no cash flow. Its price in dollars either goes up or down.

Many of the S&P 500's companies pay dividends and the appreciation calculations I used did not include them or the gains generated by reinvesting the dividends. If they had, then the S&P 500's performance above inflation would be even significantly more impressive.

Similarly, real estate's appreciation above inflation would be much more impressive if we include rents earned if the property is an investment property or the rents saved if the property is owner occupied. If we consider stock dividends and rents in our calculations, then both S&P 500 stocks and real estate easily outperform gold in appreciation.

However, there are some important caveats to the S&P 500's superior record against inflation. The index suffers from what's called "survivorship bias" because it does not reflect the stocks of companies that went bankrupt or fell out of the S&P due to poor performance. It's an important point: Since the year 2000 more than half of S&P 500 companies had been replaced by 2020.

The constantly changing composition of the S&P 500 is why it is so difficult to match its performance with other asset classes. Even though you are in an index fund, it is impossible to get the best price on a stock when every other fund is buying it as it is being added to the S&P 500 or selling it when it is being evicted.

Likewise, real estate has some real-world shortcomings. If the considerable monetary and psychological costs associated with real estate – everything from difficult tenants and clogged toilets to property taxes – are factored into our calculations, then its performance also doesn't look nearly as impressive.

So that is both the beauty and the curse of gold. It just sits there in a vault. Your biggest worry is to keep someone from stealing it – maybe even the government. But you don't have to worry about some tenant falling off a balcony or the CEO of a company you're invested in embezzling the employees' pension plan.

Liquidity

History has shown over and over that when governments become desperate for wealth, they will confiscate yours. Once the authorities sense the populace is evading their wealth confiscation schemes, capital controls – like transaction taxes or overt bans against moving wealth across borders – quickly pop up.

This tyrannical fact of financial life is why liquidity is such an important attribute for our inflation hedges. Liquidity allows us to move quickly in out of our hedge as circumstances dictate. It allows us to quickly move into cash to buy distressed assets or to potentially move our wealth out of failing and/or corrupt jurisdictions.

Cryptocurrencies are the world's most liquid and mobile assets. As of this writing they can be traded in 24-hour markets and can be bought, sold or transferred internationally with a few keystrokes.

Of course, this ease of liquidity can be destroyed if the world's governments decide to increase regulations and restrictions on cryptocurrencies. Already, long before the FTX scandal broke, there has been an increasing chorus from critics to crack down on cryptocurrencies. Increased regulation could strangle the liquidity of cryptocurrencies if their markets are forced to comply with the onerous reporting requirements afflicting other financial institutions.

Equities are also very liquid the vast majority of the time – when the stock markets are open. Liquidity is limited when the markets are closed on weekends or for holidays or revolutions. There are extended hours of trading before and after stock markets open. But liquidity is also limited during market crashes when everyone is selling and/or if trading is halted because a sudden severe drop triggers automatic market closures.

Equities are portable in so much that as long as you have a smartphone and wi-fi access you can liquidate your portfolio in seconds. However, moving the liquidated funds out of the country entails the same problems as moving cash or your bank account. The transactions are easily tracked and can be halted quickly by the authorities with a few taps on the keyboard.

Precious metals are also very liquid. You could go to your local pawn shop, coin store or "We Buy Gold" franchise and sell your gold. These places will definitely lowball you, but in an emergency, you should be able to get cash quickly. If you want a better price, try placing an ad on Craigslist or eBay. Just watch out for scammers and criminals.

Gold and silver are also effective barters and can be easily traded for goods and services. Gold is highly portable. You can literally carry several thousand dollars of it in your pocket. Be careful trying to move it out of the country, though. Border guards will be looking for it and it can easily be detected by a metal detector.

If you have ever bought or sold a house, you know that real estate is extremely illiquid. The whole process can take months and involves realtors, bankers, title agents, appraisers, inspectors, attorneys, contractors, etc. Real estate, obviously, is not portable. It would be easier to change your country's government than to move your real estate out of your country.

Durability

Gold is, without a doubt, the most durable of our inflation hedges. A treasure hunter could pull a gold coin out of a 500-year-old shipwreck lying at the bottom of the ocean and after a quick wipe with a rag it will be as brilliant as the day it was struck. Gold is mostly inert, which means it does not react with oxygen, water or just about anything else. That's why it does not rust, tarnish or burn.

Gold's melting point is 1948 °F, which is a few hundred degrees hotter than most house fires. Even if your gold did melt, once it cooled back into a solid state you could recover it. It might be in the shape of a puddle instead of a coin or bar, but all of the gold would be there. In fact, the temperature at which gold is vaporized into a gas, a.k.a. its boiling point, is 5378 °F. So, short of a direct nuclear strike or a super nova, you will always be able to recover it.

The half-life of gold is unknown but it is thought to be infinite. Even if it is not, it will be around a lot longer than you, me, the Earth or any remnant of human civilization. It is the ultimate renewable resource that can be used and reused an infinite number of times.

For example, the gold used in dentistry, electronics, aerospace, etc., can be recovered, melted down and reshaped into its next productive iteration. Suffice it to say, gold is super durable. You never have to worry about it being destroyed or consumed ... just stolen or confiscated.

Real estate has a mixed durability profile. Land is fairly durable but natural disaster, environmental contamination or crime can make it unusable. Buildings require constant upkeep and if neglected for even a short time they can become irreversibly uninhabitable. Buildings can also be destroyed by fires, floods, hurricanes, etc. Fortunately, insurance exists to make you at least partially whole if disaster strikes.

Equities are durable in the sense there is nothing really tangible to wear out or be destroyed. It's not like we have paper stock certificates anymore. Sure, the assets of the companies that you have invested in are susceptible to all of the same risks as real estate, but that is a headache for the executives of the company, not you. Of course, this lack of responsibility also means lack of control over the company, and this trade-off can have other repercussions.

Tax and Political Treatment
When you include all of the statutes, IRS regulations and court decisions, the U.S. Internal Revenue Code is over 70,000 pages long. It is so long no one knows the exact size. But what most people do not realize is that the reason the tax code is so gigantic is because the vast majority of it is tax loopholes.

If it were not for all the loopholes the federal tax code could fit on one line: "Income will be taxed at such and such rate." That is all the space it would need. But over the decades politicians have continually added loopholes and carveouts for their cronies and donors. Fortunately for us, we can also take advantage of the literally thousands of loopholes buried in the tax code.

I have neither the expertise nor the wherewithal to give even a cursory summation of the tax code, except to say that, of all our inflation hedges, real estate has by far the most favorable tax treatment. Thanks to the lobbying efforts of the National Association of Realtors, the tax code is riddled with loopholes like the mortgage deduction, the depreciation deduction, the 1031 Exchange, opportunity zone preferential treatment, the stepped-up basis for capital gains avoidance, etc.

Precious metals and equities do share in real estate's reduced capital gains tax rate if they are held for more than a year. Short-term capital gains are taxed at the rate of your ordinary tax bracket.

But long-term gains for assets held for more than a year are taxed at rates of 0%, 15% and 20% depending on your income and filing status, and this is typically less than the tax for short-term capital gains. In the state of Utah, gold and silver are considered legal tender and therefore not subject to capital gains, at least for state taxes.

Precious metals have a vibrant black market, so an investor could theoretically sell or barter some of his gold or silver and not report the capital gain. Now, I would strongly advise against this because it is illegal and could result in severe monetary penalties and/or jail time.

A free word of advice: **PAY YOUR TAXES.** Especially since there are so many legal ways to minimize the taxman's take.

Summary

In this chapter we examined how well the inflation hedges of gold, stocks and real estate embody the attributes of the perfect inflation hedge:

- ☐ Store of value
- ☐ Income producing
- ☐ Liquidity/Portability
- ☐ Durability
- ☐ Favorable tax and political treatment

None of the inflation hedges we studied possessed all of these qualities and they each had their own plusses and minuses: **Store of Value:** During the high inflation period of 1971-1981, gold was the undisputed champion with an increase in purchasing power of 322%. This is consistent with other historical high inflation periods. Real estate, as measured by median home price, increased in purchasing power by 22%. And stocks as measured by the S&P 500 had a decrease in purchasing power of −41%.

However, in the 50-year time period of 1971-2021, with inflation ranging from high to low, stocks performed the best with a 653% increase in purchasing power. Gold also performed well with an increase in purchasing power of 558% and real estate's increase was a respectable 146%.

Income Production: Real estate has the best income producing potential, but it does come with all of the headaches and costs associated with real estate ownership. Stocks can produce headache-free income in the form of dividends, but typically it's at a much lower level than real estate. Gold can produce income with the utilization of advanced financial instruments, but for the scope of this book, gold has no cash flow. In fact, many consider gold to have a negative cash flow since you often have to pay to store it.

Liquidity/Portability: Gold is highly liquid and can be easily sold or bartered. Gold is also highly portable and at $1800 an ounce just 35 pounds of it would be worth about $1 million. Stocks are highly liquid and can be easily sold as long as the stock market is open and functioning. However, many red flags would be raised if you attempted to transfer all of the contents of your brokerage account out of the country, especially during a financial crisis. Real estate is both illiquid and non-portable.

Durability: Gold is, for all intents and purposes, indestructible. Stocks and real estate are equally susceptible to the elements and environment that they inhabit.

Tax and Political Treatment: Real estate and stocks are the politically correct inflation hedges. Real estate also has a ton of favorable tax loopholes. Gold is the politically incorrect inflation hedge. Gold hoarders are generally – and unfairly – suspected of being tax evaders and/or right-wing nut jobs. Overall, I consider gold to be the best traditional inflation hedge. It has the best track record of preserving and increasing purchasing power during high inflation. It is also highly liquid with sales that can be performed outside the view of a criminal or oppressive government. Although it may take some subterfuge and intrigue, gold can be transported outside of the country during times of crisis.

Chapter 6

How to Use Loans to Get Rich Off Inflation

Leverage is the reason some people become rich and others do not become rich. –Robert Kiyosaki

In Chapter 5 we discussed how to defend against inflation by avoiding certain investments and using traditional inflation hedges. Now it is time to go on the offensive and learn how to get rich off inflation by borrowing money and investing it in assets that will hold their value over time.

As we learned in Chapter 1, inflation is a tax. Which leads us to a choice. We can either be the taxpayer or the tax collector. You might think it is immoral to get rich at the expense of the little guy, but the bitter truth is that the little guy is going to pay the inflation tax regardless of your participation.

The way I see it, it's immoral to allow only the political and financial elites to benefit from inflation. If enough ordinary like-minded people get rich off inflation, perhaps we can influence the system so it stops screwing the working stiff.

We have seen how the value of the U.S. dollar has continued its inexorable downward march for over a century. Sure, there have been degrees of the rate of its descent, but every year the dollar is worth less and less. After a century of inflation three 1913 pennies can buy what a 2022 dollar can today. Inflation is now official government policy.

They don't even try to hide it anymore. The Federal Reserve's openly stated policy is to achieve a 2% annual inflation rate, and there's talk of increasing it to 3%. We may have short bouts of deflation, but it's safe to say that over the long-term inflation will continue to compound.

Now we know there is no such thing as a sure bet. But when the government of the most powerful country in the world tells you it is going to create inflation – and the only thing it has to do to create it is to print money and send out checks to the voters – that is about as close to a sure thing as you will ever get.

If the head coach of one of the teams playing in the Super Bowl went on national TV and stated his team was going to try and intentionally lose the game, could you use the information to your advantage? Of course, you could. Bettors would be rappelling off roofs of casinos to make bets on the opposing team.

Well, that's exactly what is happening in the case of inflation. The chairman of the Federal Reserve is telling us that he's throwing the game and that inflation is going to win. So, let's use this information to craft what I call "inflation wealth generators" to grow our net worth and achieve financial independence.

The Ingredients of a Successful
Inflation Wealth Generator (IWG)

Simply put, leverage is borrowing funds to invest in an asset or enterprise. Not all credit provides suitable leverage to harness inflation. It is clear that a loan must possess certain attributes that allow it to transform inflation into wealth. The ingredients that make a loan a successful inflation wealth generator are as follows: Low Fixed-Interest Rate, Long Term, No Maintenance

Requirement for Collateral, Preferential Political/Legal Treatment and Preferential Tax Treatment.

Low Fixed-Interest Rate –The interest rate needs to be fixed and low. If a creditor has the ability to adjust the interest rate, he will do so the first opportunity he gets when the real interest rate turns low or negative. After all, they made the loan to increase their future purchasing power, not lower it. However, with a fixed-interest-rate loan inflation could skyrocket and the real interest rate could turn severely negative but the creditor would have no recourse.

A low relative interest rate to inflation is mandatory. Your interest rate does not need to be lower than inflation (i.e., negative real interest rate). As long as your interest rate is not significantly higher than inflation and your rate is fixed, the increase in your equity will soon overtake your interest expense. Also, a seemingly high interest rate may be relatively low if inflation is also high. For example, a 20% interest rate is relatively low if the inflation rate is 25%.

Long Term – When it comes to safely using leverage to profit from inflation, the longer the time horizon the better. Prices do not go up in a straight line. Inflation is punctuated by significant bouts of deflation. We must be able to borrow cash long enough so that the price declines on our leveraged assets have time to recover and return to price increases. Aside from some admittedly severe but brief spurts of deflation, the dollar's devaluation has occurred reliably for over a hundred years. You just have to stay in the game long enough to profit from its decline.

No Maintenance Requirement for Collateral – One of the reasons margin loans on your stock portfolio are so dangerous is that you are required to maintain the value of your collateral. If the value of your collateral, your stock portfolio, drops, then you have to deposit dollars into your account or sell some of your stocks to pay back a portion of the loan. But in a market crash dollars are in short supply, which means you will have to sell your stocks at a huge discount with the potential for huge losses.

To profit from inflation I recommend a loan that simply requires that you make your payment to remain in good standing. Even if the value of your collateral drops, or even if your equity turns negative, you are still only expected to make the minimum payment. Provided you can make the minimum payment and your loan term is long enough, then you can wait out deflationary periods indefinitely knowing that inflationary riches lie on the other side.

Preferential Political/Legal Treatment – Good political standing is another important attribute of leverage. Friendly political support translates into subsidies, tax deductions and legal protection. Preferential political treatment provides not only favorable laws in the present, but also provides for protection from potentially draconian laws in the future when things inevitably get bad.

Preferential political treatment inevitably leads to preferential legal treatment. The benefit of a friendly court adjudicating your dispute with a creditor cannot be overstated. A court decision can determine your solvency or, if necessary, the terms of your bankruptcy.

Preferential Tax Treatment – Preferential tax treatment is a subset of preferential political/legal treatment. Obviously, we want our loan to have tax advantages. That is, we want interest payments and fees to be tax deductible. Interest payments are a tax-deductible business expense. Also, interest on loans to fund investments are deductible against your net investment income. Interest on loans used to buy rental properties can be deducted against the rental income generated by the rental properties.

Interest on personal consumption expenses, like credit card interest or auto loan interest, is not deductible with the notable exception of the mortgage interest expense on your primary home. You can deduct your mortgage interest on the first $750,000 of your mortgage.

Summary

The preferred attributes of leverage that are needed to be an effective inflation wealth generator are as follows:

- ☐ Low Fixed Interest Rate
- ☐ Long Term
- ☐ No Maintenance Requirement for Collateral
- ☐ Preferential Tax Treatment
- ☐ Preferential Legal Treatment

Fortunately, there is a form of leverage that possesses all of these qualities. It is a common and politically acceptable inflation hedge. It is a form of leverage that has generated outsized gains for millions of people without them even really understanding why. This superstar of leverage is, of course, the home mortgage.

Chapter 7

The Home Mortgage – King of the Wealth Generators

If I knew where I was going to want to live the next five or 10 years, I would buy a home and I'd finance it with a 30-year mortgage ... It's a terrific deal. —Warren Buffett

The home mortgage is the best inflation wealth generator most people never knew they had. Ordinary people from all income levels have been generating wealth from their home mortgage completely unaware that inflation has been increasing the nominal value of their home and subsequently their equity reliably every year.

Today people in California and other expensive real estate areas are selling their modest multimillion-dollar homes, moving to low-cost states, buying similar accommodations and comfortably retiring on the proceeds of their sale.

If you were to ask them how they did it, the vast majority would not have a clue. Sure, they would say they made a killing in real estate. But what they would not know is that it was really their mortgage that generated their wealth, not their home. Their mortgage had all of the criteria necessary for it to be a super inflation wealth generator.

The Home Mortgage Checks All the Boxes

The common 30-year fixed home mortgage checks all the criteria needed to be an effective inflation wealth generator:

Low Fixed Interest Rate – At the time of this writing, in late 2022, inflation had climbed to a little over 8 percent and interest rates for home mortgages had spiked to over 7 percent. But in early 2022 the vast majority of borrowers could get a mortgage at less than 4%. For the most qualified home buyers it was under 3%. Incredibly, these interest rates are fixed for up to 30 years at a time when the CPI had already climbed over 6%. It is also interesting that despite mortgage rates increasing significantly in late 2022, they are still less than the rate of inflation and are therefore negative.

Bear in mind that the only reason this great loan deal is possible is because home mortgages are subsidized and guaranteed by the government. No one would ever loan their own capital for 30 years for 3%, especially when the Federal Reserve's announced inflation target is at least 2%. Assuming only, a 2% inflation rate, the very best a lender could hope for is a 1% real return – and that's assuming your borrower can make the payments.

If inflation rises above 3%, then your real interest rate goes negative and you are locked in for up to 30 years. What if, God forbid, inflation hit 10% or 15%? Well, even if that level of inflation is not sustained the purchasing power of what you have lent out is going to be a lot less than what you got paid back.

Government sponsored enterprises (GSEs) like Fannie Mae and Freddie Mac purchase and guarantee conforming loans in the secondary markets. They are private organizations but have an implied guarantee from the federal government and were bailed out during the 2008 Financial Crisis.

Without GSEs the interest rate of the typical mortgage would be triple or quadruple what it is now. Creditors would be very cautious about the risk of inflation and would only lend at a variable rate that is indexed to some marker of inflation. Any fixed-rate loan would be very short term (a year or less) with a balloon payment at the end.

You only have to look at the hard-money lending market to see that the typical interest rate for a loan is between 10% and 15%. Hard money lenders are not eligible for loan guarantees and therefore they are unwilling to lend their capital without an interest rate that is commensurate with the risk of default and inflation.

Long Terms – Another essential quality for an inflation wealth generator is a term long enough to smooth out any brief periods of deflation. Remember, deflation is the kryptonite of leverage. If deflation is deep and protracted, even the most solvent of debtors will go bust.

The vast majority of home mortgages have 15- or 30-year terms. The average business cycle, the time between recessions, is approximately five years. So, a 30-year term will give you ample time to recover from even the most serious bouts of deflation. A 15-year term is probably fine, but if you have high inflation expectations my advice is to always take the longest term possible even if it means a slightly higher interest rate.

No Maintenance Requirements for Collateral – The absence of maintenance requirements for collateral is necessary to avoid being forced to sell at market lows. As mentioned before, with a margin loan your stock portfolio is the collateral and you are required to maintain the value of that collateral.

If the value of your stock portfolio decreases significantly, say during a stock market crash, you either have to sell off some of your portfolio to pay down the loan or deposit cash to your account to increase the value your collateral. If you are forced to sell during the crash, you will be selling at market lows and won't participate in the gains when the market recovers. That is why I do not recommend margin loans for the vast majority of investors.

A home mortgage is very different. With a home mortgage the home you purchase is the collateral. But if the value of your house drops, the bank does not force you to sell your home or pay down the loan to keep your debt-to-equity level at 20%. There is no maintenance requirement. As long as you keep current on your mortgage and make your monthly payment, you are fine. The bank will not sell your home at fire-sale prices or demand that you bring in thousands of dollars to pay down the principal.

When I bought my first home for $540,000 in Las Vegas in October of 2008, it was ground zero for the 2008 Housing Crisis. At the time I thought I had gotten a pretty good deal. At their peak in 2006 and 2007 the houses in my neighborhood were going for up to $740,000. I figured I had bought at the bottom or close to it. I put down $108,000, a 20% down payment, and got a conventional 15-year mortgage at 5% (interest rates were higher back then).

I had been a real estate bear for probably four years before the housing crash, but even I was surprised at the ferocity of the price drop. By 2010 the market finally found a bottom and by then I had worked out how to use a mortgage as an inflation wealth generator. It seemed like a great time to start investing in real estate. I started looking at single family homes as investment properties. I had already bought three or four rental properties in the $100,000 range when I saw a foreclosed house in my neighborhood get listed for sale.

During the Housing Crisis plenty of homes in my neighborhood went into foreclosure or were short sales. But what was special about this house was that it was an exact match of my house. Well, that is not entirely true. It was not exactly the same. It was better. Instead of a great room with 20-foot ceilings, it had a loft for the kids. Instead of a side garage, it had an office. And instead of a big patio in the backyard, it had a pool! But here's the kicker: It was listed at $280,000 -- a full $260,000 less than what I had paid for my house just a year and a half earlier.

If this foreclosure was worth $280,000, by my estimate that meant the house I was living in was now worth around $250,000. This realization hit me like a punch in the face. This meant that my $108,000 down payment was gone, and since I still owed about $425,000 on the mortgage, I was underwater $175,000. If you add the $175,000 that I was underwater to my already evaporated $108,000 down payment, then my net worth took a $283,000 hit.

At the time a lot of homeowners in my situation went into foreclosure or did a short sale. Fortunately for me, my job is recession proof and I always had a steady paycheck. I was able to pay my mortgage every month. I was able to refinance at a lower rate and, as it always does, the market recovered. If I had a margin call on my mortgage and had been required to make another $104,000 down payment to the mortgage holder, I would not have been able to do it and the bank subsequently would have foreclosed on me.

As of this writing, my house is now worth a conservative $750,000 with a mortgage balance of about $315,000. That gives me equity of $435,000 -- quadruple my down payment. Granted, I was paying interest expenses, property taxes, insurances, maintenance, etc., but I also did not have a rent payment. I will take quadrupling my initial investment in 12 years and having a great place to live all day long.

I bought at nearly the worst time. Even though my collateral had dropped in value by over 50%, the bank was not able foreclose or demand that I pay down the loan. I just had to make my monthly mortgage payment, which I did. And as a result, I was able to reap the benefit of a rising real estate market.

Preferential Political/Legal Treatment – Home ownership is the politically correct inflation hedge whereas owning gold is seditious. Tell people that you have a gold hoard buried somewhere in your backyard and you will be probably end up on a domestic terrorist list somewhere. But buying a house ... that is the American Dream. And no one is ever going to quibble with a private citizen taking out a mortgage to buy his own little slice of Americana.

Leverage tools like a margin loan, an auto loan and credit card debt typically do not get preferential legal treatment. For example, the terms and conditions of a margin loan are clearly stated. Your brokerage can and will force the sale of your securities to make itself whole. Even if you tried litigating to recover your repossessed equities, it is unlikely that a court would look favorably on a greedy speculator that got burned by a crashing market.

A home mortgage borrower however, tends to find sympathy in most courts. Judges do not like kicking people out of their homes, even if they are clearly in default, and they usually give the homeowner ample opportunity to become current with their mortgage.

Creditors know this and they will often voluntarily restructure a loan to more favorable terms for the mortgage borrower. These concessions typically take the form of forbearance, interest-only payments, increasing the length of the term, lowering the rate or even reducing the principal. As we saw in the 2008 financial crisis, when widespread downturn occurs, many government and private programs will pop up to assist or outright bailout mortgage borrowers in default.

Preferential Tax Treatment – Home ownership is encouraged at all levels of government. It is thought that homeowners are more invested and engaged in their communities and therefore make better citizens. Because home ownership is looked upon so favorably, it receives preferential tax treatment. At least that is the official reason for the preferential tax treatment. The cynical reason is that realty and home building interests bribe our elected officials with political contributions to get them to legislate these tax breaks, which politicians then use to bribe voters. Regardless, these tax breaks are not going anywhere any time soon.

The most notable tax breaks for homeowners and real estate investors are the mortgage interest deduction and the 1031 exchange. But these are far from being the only tax incentives. There is also the Section 121 Exclusion, Opportunity Zone investing, stepped up cost basis and thousands more loopholes, grants, subsidies, exclusions, etc., buried in the federal and state tax codes.

Because of the complexity and ever-changing nature of the tax code, I recommend consulting qualified tax and real estate professionals for your real estate tax needs. As I've said, I do not possess the expertise nor the wherewithal to give more than a cursory summation of the preferential tax treatment homeownership is afforded. In the sections below I have included an introduction to the most common real estate tax loopholes in the tax code: The home mortgage deduction, stepped-up cost basis, 1031 exchanges and the Section 121 exclusion.

Home Mortgage Deduction -- One of the most popular of all tax deductions in the federal tax code, the home mortgage deduction is used by millions of taxpayers each year to reduce their tax burdens. The home mortgage deduction allows you to deduct your mortgage interest on the first $750,000 of your mortgage. For the vast majority of Americans that covers 100% of their loan. This deduction lowers the cost of the loan, which is materially the same as lowering the interest rate. For most homeowners this makes their real interest rate go from negative to even more negative.

Step-Up in Basis Provision -- "Cost basis" is the original purchase price of the asset. Capital gains are calculated by subtracting the cost basis from the sales price. Capital gains are then taxed at your ordinary tax bracket. The step-up basis provision "steps up" the cost basis of an inherited asset to the date when the decedent dies. So, when you die, your heirs' cost basis is the value of the asset when they inherit it and not when you purchased it.

For example, let's say you bought a home for $500,000 and when you died it was worth $1,000,000. Your children inherit it and sell it a year later for $1.1 million. For tax purposes, the cost basis of the home is "stepped up" to its fair market value on the date you died, which was $1 million, and not $500,000, the cost you paid for it. Your kids' capital gain is only $100,000 and not $600,000. If they are in the highest tax bracket of 37% that is a difference between a tax bill of $37,000 versus $222,000.

1031 Exchange – A 1031 exchange allows you defer tax on capital gains on investment real estate provided you owned the property for at least two years and you purchase a similar property for at least as much as you sold your previous property. 1031 exchanges have very specific requirements and you must adhere to a strict timeline. I recommend using a qualified real estate professional to guide you through the process, but the basics are illustrated in the following example:

If you bought a rental property for $500,000 and sold it for $1 million, you realized a $500,000 capital gain. You can defer capital gains taxes by purchasing another home for at least $1 million dollars within 180 days. You can continue to do 1031 exchanges and defer capital gains taxes indefinitely.

And if you die before winding down your 1031 exchange your heirs will pay tax on a much smaller capital gain because of the step-up in basis provision (see the above section.) This is the case regardless of how many 1031 exchanges you do or how large your capital gains are. You could potentially realize millions in capital gains from scores of 1031 exchanges and your heirs could inherit all of your lifetime capital gains tax free. They say the only certainties in this world are death and taxes, but in this case your death legally cheats the tax man.

Section 121 Exclusion -- The Section 121 exclusion allows the seller of a home to realize up to $250,000 (if single) or up to $500,000 (if married filing jointly) on the capital gains from the sale of their primary residence tax free. The property does not have to be the primary residence at the time it was sold. It just has to be the seller's primary residence for 24 out of the last 60 months. The 24 months do not have to be continuous and the capital gains do not have to be reinvested like they do for a 1031 exchange. The proceeds from this sale can literally be spent on anything.

Summary

The home mortgage possesses qualities that make it the best inflation wealth generator in existence:

- ☐ Low fixed rates that become negative real rates when inflation is high.
- ☐ Long terms that allow the investor to ride out steep bouts of deflation.
- ☐ No maintenance requirement of collateral – no additional funds beyond the minimum monthly payment are required to remain current even if deflation wipes out investor equity.
- ☐ Homeownership, and by extension the home mortgage, is the politically correct hedge against inflation. In fact, it is encouraged by all levels of government and society at large.

☐ The legal system is sympathetic toward the homeowner and will make allowances to keep the homeowner in his home. A delinquent homeowner is typically given ample opportunity to become current including favorable changes to the principal, rate and term.

☐ The tax code is rife with tax breaks and incentives for homeownership and the home mortgage.

The Wrong Types of Leverage

Warren Buffet is famously quoted as saying, "There are three ways a smart person can go broke... 'liquor, ladies and leverage.'" He went on to clarify that it is actually only leverage that makes you go broke. Why? Because while it is true that leverage multiplies your profit during good times, it also multiplies your losses during the bad times. If you are overleveraged, then even very small downturns can cause insolvency. (Bankruptcy is really Nature's way of telling you that you are overleveraged.)

As we have seen, you can make a fortune using leverage to profit from inflation, but not just any type of leverage will do. Only very specific types of leverage can be inflation wealth generators. The trick is to find the right type of leverage to use to buy the right type of asset.

Using the wrong type of leverage – buying stocks on margin, for instance – will usually end with you going broke. Buying on margin is when you borrow cash from your own brokerage account and use the cash and the securities already in your account as collateral to buy more securities.

Buying on margin is very tempting. For a relatively low interest rate, a typical brokerage house will let you borrow up to 100% of the value of your account. So, for example, if your securities are worth $1,000, then you can borrow $1,000 from your broker and the total value of your account is now $2,000.

Your equity in the account is still $1,000 but you now have an additional $1,000 to invest in stocks. Any profit you make on the borrowed $1,000 is yours, but so is any loss. If you lose money, you have to pay the borrowed $1,000 back in full with interest.

The catch to this sweet-looking deal is that you must have a certain amount of equity in your brokerage account at all times. This is called the maintenance requirement. If your equity drops below the maintenance requirement, then you have a short period of time to increase your collateral. You can do that either by depositing cash into your account or selling some of your securities until your equity fulfills the maintenance requirement.

This is what's called a margin call, which is essentially the brokerage calling in a percentage of its loan to you and having you pay down the principal. If you fail to meet the maintenance requirement on time, your brokerage will sell off your securities until you do.

It should be clear from this arrangement that your stockbroker is not your silent partner. It is your creditor, and a tough one. Your broker can and will change your maintenance requirement and interest rate at any time, usually at the moment that inflicts maximum financial pain.

Because stocks can and do drop precipitously in a very short time, buying on margin can be a very risky way to invest. It's an easy way to lose a lot of money quickly, especially when the stock market crashes. It has personally happened to me twice. The first time was immediately after the 9/11 terrorist attack and the second time was during the COVID-19 pandemic crash in March of 2020.

To understand the precariousness of buying on margin, let's look at a fictional investor named Nancy. Nancy is new to investing but she has viewed hundreds of TikTok videos of people getting rich in the stock market. Nancy opens a brokerage account and deposits $1,000.

She is inpatient to grow her wealth and gets a margin loan from her broker for another $1,000. She then invests all of the funds into the stock market – a total of $2,000 with $1,000 in equity and $1,000 in a margin loan. Her maintenance agreement requires her to maintain a 50% equity position in her account.

The next day the stock market crashes and the value of Nancy's account drops 10% and is now worth $1,800. She still owes the brokerage the $1,000 loan, so it is her equity that is decreased by $200 to $800. Her equity in her account value only dropped by 20% ($200), but her loan amount stayed the same.

Since Nancy has no available cash to add to her account to meet her 50% maintenance requirement, she must sell $200 worth of her securities to meet it. After they are sold her account value sinks to $1,600 ($800 in equity + $800 in the margin loan). Her $800 in equity now fulfills the 50% maintenance requirement.

Unfortunately for Nancy, however, thousands of other investors have gotten similar margin calls and when the market opens in the morning, it immediately begins to sell off. The value of the stocks in her account fall another 20% – $320 – to $1,280. That means her equity of $800 drops another $320 or 40% to $480 ($1,280 total account value - $800 margin loan = $480).

Then Nancy receives an urgent text message from her broker that informs her that her account has been liquidated to pay her $800 margin loan, but she still has a $320 deficit ($800 - $480 = $320). The brokerage tells her that if she fails to pay the $320 in 48 hours, they will begin legal proceedings.

Witnessing her account's equity drop to $0 in just two days, Nancy, demoralized, decides to close her account. She is out of the market for good and vows never to invest in the stock market again, believing it is "rigged" against the little guy.

A week or so later, the Federal Reserve and U.S. Congress launched massive monetary and fiscal stimulus that resulted in the stock market recovering all of its losses and making new highs. Unfortunately for Nancy, she did not realize any of those gains. If she had not been forced to sell her stocks at the bottom and simply held on to them, she would have had positive gains.

I wish I could tell you that Nancy's disastrous experience with buying on margin is an exaggeration or an anomaly, but it is not. Every time there is a market crash, overleveraged investors must sell into a falling market, which then fuels even further price declines. The additional price drops force investors who were less leveraged than the first wave of investors to sell. This vicious downward spiral sucks more and more leveraged investors into its vortex until the market finally bottoms or gets bailed out by the Federal Reserve and/or the government.

The problem with stock margin loans is that the terms of your maintenance requirement are not fixed. Your broker can increase the interest rate on your loan if inflation ramps up or increase your equity maintenance requirement if stock prices plummet or market volatility spikes.

If you did not understand the financial process of the above example, do not worry. The only thing you really need to know is to never buy stocks on margin. If you need further proof of the risk of buying on margin, remember the case of a hypothetical investor who invested in Warren Buffet's Berkshire Hathaway fund in 1964.

Buffet's famously successful fund has experienced consistently high annual return over the last 57 years. But if in 1964 our investor had invested $500 of his own money and borrowed another $500 in a margin loan from his broker to invest $1,000 in Berkshire Hathaway stock he would have been completely wiped out by margin calls on at least four different occasions. If he had simply invested his own $500 and not borrowed any money from his broker on margin, his $500 would be worth nearly $18 million today.

Advanced Studies: When a brokerage makes a margin loan, they are increasing the money supply in the stock market – not unlike when a bank makes a mortgage loan for someone buying a house. The margin loan is inflationary because it pumps money into the market and leads to higher stock prices. When the brokerage raises its maintenance requirements or forces a margin call, it is reducing the money supply and taking money out of the market. That is deflationary and causes stock prices to drop.

Other Types of Bad Leverage

Any type of credit that has a short term (less than 5 years), variable interest rate, positive real interest rate or is used to buy a depreciating asset is the wrong type of leverage. This includes auto loans, adjustable-rate mortgages or payday loans.

The 0% credit card balance transfer/cash advance can be a quick way of obtaining a very low interest rate, usually for 12 to 18 months. But this type of leverage is not suitable for most people. These are teaser rates and then after the specified time the interest rates go sky high. These rates are variable, so credit card companies can adjust them higher if inflation ratchets up.

Also, some debtors continually pay off one 0% credit card balance with another 0% credit card offer just before it expires. Just remember, this works only until there is a financial crisis and/or high inflation. When this happens, those 0% balance transfer offers will cease to exist.

If you are a sophisticated investor and have the ability to pay off your credit card once the teaser rate expires, the 0% credit card can be away of obtaining a short-term very low interest rate. Just be careful because the length of the promotional 0% interest rate is not long enough to profit from inflation.

Summary

Credit that has a positive real rate of interest, variable rate or short term is not suitable as leverage to function as an inflation wealth generator. Margin loans on stock portfolios should be avoided at all costs because the volatility in a financial crisis could lead to margin calls and deep losses and sometimes even to the complete liquidation of the portfolio.

Chapter 8

Home Mortgage Scenarios

*Homes – the very idea of homeownership – evoke a strong
emotional reaction in all of us.* –Spencer Rascoff

Remember Dr. Spendthrift? He was our big spending 35-year-old
physician from Chapter 4 who had a miraculous wealth turnaround
thanks to the wealth-creating power of inflation.

In this chapter we'll take a closer look at his fictional story and
see exactly how the wealth-creating power of the home mortgage
saved him from drowning in $4 million in debt and made him so
wealthy he was able to retire like a duke.

Dr. Spendthrift's reversal of fortune occurred because
inflation relentlessly ate away at his mortgage debt for 30 years,
leaving him with millions of dollars of newly minted net worth.
Recall that he had a high annual income of $500,000. He also
had a combined $4 million in mortgage debt from his primary
residence and two vacation homes and $100,000 in student debt
(Table 2). Fortunately for Dr. Spendthrift, his heavy debt, which
at first seemed like an anchor, became a lifeline.

In the following sections we will devise scenarios and crunch
the numbers to illustrate how the home mortgage harnesses
inflation to generate significant wealth for the mortgage borrower
– that's you.

In these scenarios all loans are non-amortizing, have no down payment and have a balloon principal payment due at the end of the term. We will not consider the mortgage-rate tax deductions or other benefits of homeownership. Also, to simplify things, we won't consider property tax, maintenance expenses and all the other expenses associated with homeownership.

In our first scenario we examine the mechanics of how Dr. Spendthrift got rich. Specifically, we will show how his mortgage debt became an increasingly smaller percentage of the value of his portfolio and his mortgage interest payments became an increasingly smaller percentage of his salary.

Thought Experiment 1

Dr. Spendthrift Gets Rich. Moderate Inflation and Negative Real Interest Rates.

Initial Conditions: Year 2023

- Inflation = 10%
- Home value and income increase at the exact rate of inflation
- 30-year home mortgage at 7% APR fixed
- Real interest rate = -3%

Real Estate Price 2023	Mortgage Debt 2023	% Mortgage to Price
$4,000,000	$4,000,000	100%

Equity = $0

Real Estate Price 2053	Mortgage Debt 2053	% Mortgage to Price
$69,797,608	$4,000,000	5.7%

Nominal Equity = $65,797,608
Real Equity = $3,770,765.73 (in 2023 dollars)

On the surface it appears that Dr. Spendthrift became a multimillionaire because his properties increased in price. After 30 years the price of his properties increased to a combined value of $69,797,608, but in real terms their values did not increase. After adjusting for inflation, their value had the exact amount of purchasing power they had 30 years earlier. It took the same amount of purchasing power to buy the properties in both 2023 and 2043. So, what happened? How did he become rich?

The big increase in the nominal price of Dr. Spendthrift's properties is only half of the equation. The other half is that the annual 10% inflation rate lowered the real cost of his mortgage principal and interest payments, both of which were fixed. For 30 years his debt was fixed at $4 million, but $4 million dollars buys a lot less in 2053 than it did in 2023. After 30 years, inflation reduced the real cost of his mortgages to $229,234 (in 2023 dollars).

And that's it. That's the secret to Dr. Spendthrift's success. His properties kept up with inflation, but his debt didn't.

After 30 years of 7% inflation, his properties still had a real value of $4 million (in 2023 dollars), but inflation reduced the real cost of his mortgages to $229,234 (in 2023 dollars) resulting in a stunning increase of nearly $4 million in real net worth. Dr. Spendthrift's fixed-rate mortgage harnessed inflation and made him rich.

Dr. Spendthrift's salary kept up exactly with inflation. As per his employment contract, he got a cost-of-living adjustment equal to the rate of inflation. His starting salary was $500,000/year and after 30 years of 10% inflation his salary increased to $8,724,701/year. Keep in mind that the purchasing power of his salary remained the same.

In contrast, the annual interest on his fixed 7% mortgages was $280,000. And after 30 years of 10% inflation the annual interest rate is still $280,000. In 2023 Dr. Spendthrift's mortgage interest payments were 56% of his salary ($280,000/$500,000

= .56). In 2053 his interest payments were 3.2% of his salary ($280,000/$8,724,701 = .032) (Graph 4). You can imagine how much more comfortable life got for Dr. Spendthrift.

Annual Mortgage Interest as Percent
of Salary in 2023 Dollars
(Graph 4)

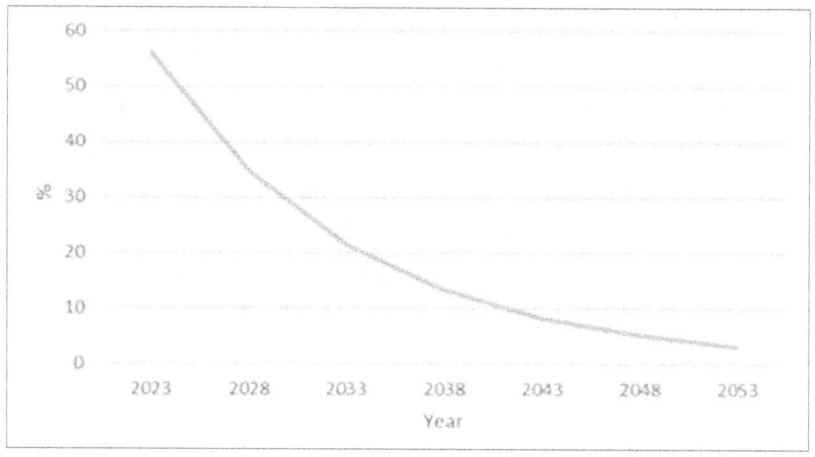

What About the Rest of Us?

You are probably thinking: That's great for Dr. Spendthrift, but I am not a high-income physician who makes half a million a year and can get mortgages totaling $4 million dollars for a primary residence and two vacation homes. What about the rest of us? What about ordinary families who work ordinary jobs and make ordinary salaries? Does the home mortgage Inflation Wealth Generator work for average, ordinary people?

While I concede that Mr. Spendthrift's economic situation is much different from most people's, inflation does not discriminate. Anyone can harness inflation's wealth generating power provided you can get a fixed, low-interest long-term loan. And that's exactly where the home mortgage comes in.

There are scores of programs at every level of government specifically designed to help people get home loans. They have programs for first-time home buyers, low-income people, minorities, women, veterans, the disabled and new home buyers with good credit, bad credit and probably no credit at all.

The government is literally falling all over itself to incentivize banks to loan hundreds of thousands of dollars to buy houses. And remember – the only reason a bank would ever loan hundreds of thousands of dollars at negative real interest rates is because the loans are heavily subsidized by the government. No one would risk their own capital for a guaranteed loss.

When I have explained the use of a mortgage as an inflation wealth strategy, people are skeptical. Their biggest misgiving is their future earnings. They have no trouble believing inflation will increase the price of everything, but they have serious doubts that their income will increase enough to realize the benefits of inflation devaluing their debts. But wages are the price of labor and, just like every other price, they will increase with inflation. In fact, rising wages are often the biggest component of inflation.

Not everyone's income will increase exactly at the rate of inflation. For some it will be less and for some it will be more. One thing is certain, however – everyone's salary will increase during inflation. If it does not, then you will quit and find one that does. We saw this with "The Great Resignation" of 2021/2022. Employees were resigning in droves and finding much higher paying jobs.

In the summer of 1989, I got my first job at my hometown McDonald's earning the minimum wage of $3.35 per hour. According to the Consumer Price Index (CPI), $3.35 in 1989 is equivalent to $8.30 in 2023. Interestingly, that same McDonald's is now offering new hires $12 per hour, which is a significant increase over the wage the CPI would predict.

As I've stated before the CPI was designed to understate

inflation. Nevertheless, it can be safely said that even the wages of entry-level positions like a McDonald's hamburger flipper have at least kept pace with inflation. And although their wages and the mortgages are not as large as our fictional friends Dr. Frugal and Dr. Spendthrift, ordinary people in the real world can use their home mortgage as an inflation wealth generator.

Let's conduct another thought experiment, only this time we'll use more realistic inputs. Instead of a $500,000 annual income we will use $62,000, the approximate U.S. median household income. And, instead of a $4 million real estate portfolio we will consider a $300,000 single-family home.

Thought Experiment 2

Average Joe Creates Wealth. Moderate Inflation and Negative Real Interest Rates. No Real Home Value Gains.

Like the previous thought experiment, we assume a moderate annual inflation rate of 10%, and we assume that home values, salaries, and rents increase at the same rate as inflation. As with our previous thought experiment, the mortgage is non-amortizing, with no down payment and a balloon principal payment is due at the end of the 30-year term and fixed at 7%.

Initial Conditions: Year 2023

- Inflation = 10%
- Home value and income increase at the exact rate of inflation
- 30-year home mortgage at 7% APR fixed
- Real interest rate = -3%
- Mortgage Principal = $300,000
- Interest = $1,750/month ($21,000/year)
- Rent for comparable house = $750/month ($9,000/year)
- Income = $62,000/year ($5,167/month)
- Starting Equity = $0

Meet Average Joe

Average Joe is an average guy with an average job. His annual household income is $62,000, which is the average median annual income in the United States. There is nothing exceptional about Joe. He is not particularly intelligent, ambitious or financially astute. But he is lucky.

You see, Joe unwittingly stumbled into the investment of a lifetime. An investment that will net him over half a million dollars in real wealth and savings over the next 30 years.

You're probably thinking that Average Joe got lucky and invested in the next hot start up. Nope. All he did was buy a house for $300,000 with a 30-year mortgage fixed at 7% during a period of 10% inflation.

Home Price 2023	Mortgage Debt 2023	% Mortgage to Price
$300,000	$300,000	100%

Equity = $0

Home Price 2053	Mortgage Debt 2053	% Mortgage to Price
$5,234,821	$300,000	5.7%

Nominal Equity = $4,934,821
Real Equity = $282,807 (in 2023 dollars)

In 2053, after 30 years of 10% annual increases, Joe's $300,000 home soars to an astounding price of $5,234,821. After subtracting the original $300,000 Joe still owes on the mortgage, he is left with $4,934,821 in equity. After adjusting for inflation, Joe has $282,807 (in 2023 dollars) in equity. Joe went from $0 in equity to nearly $300,000 in real inflation-adjusted equity. Not bad for an average Joe.

After 30 years, Joe's salary has increased from $5,167/month ($62,000/year) to $90,155/month ($1,081,863/year). His mortgage principal started off in 2023 being nearly five times his annual salary but ended up being about one fourth of his 2053 salary. Similarly, his original monthly mortgage payment stayed the same at $1,750. Joe's interest payment went from 34% of his income to a mere 1.94%. It went from being one of the largest line items in his budget to probably less than the cellphone bill.

You're probably thinking to yourself, "Wait a second. Joe paid a total of $630,000 in interest which more than erases his entire gain in equity."

But that is only correct if you don't adjust interest for inflation. What the skeptics are forgetting is that every month inflation is decreasing the value of the monthly $1,750 interest payment. The first $1,750 interest payment is worth a lot more than the last $1,750 interest payment 30 years later.

The inflation-adjusted value of the total interest Joe paid is just $281,590. Subtracting the inflation-adjusted interest paid ($281,590) from Joe's real equity in the property ($282,807), he is still left with a $1,217 real gain.

I will concede that $1,217 isn't much, but Joe got something else for all that interest he paid. He got a place to live for 30 years. His interest payment was fixed at $1,750/month for 30 years, but if he had to pay rent it would have increased every year. If you've ever been a tenant, you know that the landlord usually raises the rent at every lease renewal. So, what would Joe's rent be if he had rented for 30 years instead of buying his home?

Let's assume that instead of buying he initially rented his home for $750/month, less than half his monthly mortgage interest payment. But it doesn't stay at $750/month. It increases at the exact rate of inflation, and after 30 years his rent is $11,897/month and $142,768 a year, nearly seven times what his interest payment would have been if he had a mortgage. If Joe had rented instead of buying, he would have paid a total $1,480,446 in nominal rent or $270,000 in 2022 dollars.

Robert Kiyosaki and other personal finance gurus assert that your personal residence is not an asset because cash flows out the property in the form of interest, taxes, maintenance, etc., instead of cash flowing into it. But you have to live somewhere and what Mr. Kiyosaki and others fail to recognize is that by living in your home you avoid having to pay rent. You are de facto receiving income equivalent to what you would have paid in rent for an equivalent home. I don't know about you. But that sure sounds like positive cash flow to me.

So how much financial gain does Average Joe accrue by harnessing inflation with his fixed-rate mortgage home purchase? We can calculate this by adding up the benefits and subtracting the costs. To keep it simple we will only discuss it in real (inflation adjusted) terms. First, we take the final home price and add the total rent saved. Next, we subtract the total interest paid and the mortgage principal. This is illustrated by the following equation: $300,000 (Final Home Price) + $270,000 (Total Rent Saved) - $281,590 (Interest Paid) - $17,193 (Mortgage Principal) = $271,217.

All told, Average Joe's house purchase with a fixed-home mortgage coupled with inflation bestowed on him over a quarter million dollars above and beyond what he paid in interest and mortgage principal. I remind you that Joe's gain of $271,217 is in 2022 dollars. It is adjusted for inflation.

Average Joe with his average job and home managed to acquire a financial windfall. He didn't work more hours, go back to school or get promoted. He never got a real raise. His salary merely kept up with inflation. Similarly, he did not remodel his home or put in a pool. His home stayed the exact same price in real terms. It was Average Joe's fixed-rate home mortgage and inflation that created his wealth.

Sounds too good to be true, right? Well, this is exactly what happened for millions of our parents and grandparents who bought homes decades ago at what today seem like bargain basement prices, but at the time were considered exorbitant. They sold their homes decades later at even more exorbitant prices, giving them big real profits and the means to fund their retirements. Like Mr. Spendthrift and Average Joe, these retirees stepped backwards into their windfall with no awareness that it was their fixed-rate home mortgage and inflation that it was their fixed-rate home mortgage that made it all possible.

Thought Experiment 3
Opportunity Cost of Buying with Cash.

Now the naysayers among you are probably thinking, "This guy is a fraud. Rising home prices created the wealth, not the home mortgage. Wealth would have been created if Average Joe had bought the house with cash. He would have saved on rent and would not have wasted all the money on interest."

This is true, but it doesn't tell the whole story. Let's crunch the numbers (adjusted for inflation). If Average Joe had bought his home with cash, he would not have any rent or interest payments. He would have started with $300,000 in equity and ended with $300,000 in equity. But he would have saved $270,000 in rent leaving him with a net financial gain of $270,000, only $1,217 less than if he had bought his home with a mortgage.

Average Joe achieved nearly identical results regardless of whether he bought his home with cash or a mortgage. However, it is not a fair comparison. In the cash example, Average Joe started out with equity of $300,000. That's a huge advantage yet buying in cash still netted less financial gain than when Joe started with equity of $0 and used a mortgage. The superiority of using our inflation wealth generator in an inflationary environment becomes more evident when we consider what else Average Joe could have invested in with his $300,000 of cash.

Instead of using his $300,000 to purchase his home, Average Joe could invest it in a S&P 500 index fund and then use a mortgage to buy his home. So that I am not accused of cherry picking, let's assume his S&P 500 index fund obtained an average annual return of 5%, which is half the assumed rate of 10% inflation. After 30 years, the nominal value of Joe's S&P index fund is $1,296,583, but after adjusting for inflation it is only worth $74,305.

That means Average Joe's index fund has a real annual rate of return of -5%. Even though his investment increased in nominal terms, it decreased in real terms and in purchasing power. This is obviously a terrible investment on its own, but shockingly Average Joe is better off making this investment than parking his $300,000 as equity in his home. How? Let's crunch the numbers.

We already know from the previous thought experiment that when Average Joe buys a $300,000 home with a fixed-rate mortgage, he has a real financial gain of $271,217. If we add the $74,305 in real value from his index fund, we see that he has a total financial gain of $345,522, which is significantly more than the $270,00 financial gain if he bought the home with cash.

If the S&P 500 index fund had been Average Joe's sole investment, it would have been a disaster. However, despite the $300,000 investment not keeping up with inflation and losing value in real terms, it did more than quadruple in nominal terms. Instead of being dead money in the purchase of a home that could have been bought with a mortgage, the additional investment in stocks added to Joe's real financial gain.

While it is true that in the high inflation era of 1971-1981 gold, real estate and stocks all had significant increases in price, there is no guarantee this trend will continue during future periods of inflation. And I am not advising that we should mortgage our homes to the hilt and invest all the proceeds in gold or the stock market. However, in periods of high inflation, it is better to buy a home with a low-rate fixed mortgage and prudently invest the cash you would have used to buy the home in a diversified portfolio of stocks and commodities.

As stated earlier, all of our examples are just looking at the benefits of home ownership and not the many costs. It is important to remember that property taxes, maintenance costs, utilities, landscaping, etc., all increase at the pace of inflation. If these costs were figured into the equation our benefit would decrease -- and significantly in some instances.

Chapter 9

Alternatives to
the Home Mortgage

*I have a number of different options, and each one gives me
something different.* –Glen Hoddle

I hope by this point it has been made abundantly clear that the best
inflation hedge is a long-term, fixed-rate, low-interest loan used to
purchase an asset whose value will grow at least as fast as inflation.

In my opinion, a 30-year home mortgage is the best option for
most people. However, some investors may prefer other leveraged
Inflation Wealth Generators. Some investors may already own a
home and have no desire to buy a new one or become a landlord.

The problem is that other Inflation Wealth Generators are rare.
Why? Because IWGs typically have to be government subsidized.
A rational private investor would never knowingly loan money
below the rate of inflation. The only reason these other IWGs exist
is because like the home mortgage, the government subsidizes
them, and the government does not care if it loses money.

Because alternative IWGs are rare, there are only three suitable
alternatives to replace or complement the home mortgage: 1 –
Cash Out Refinancing. 2 – The Reverse Mortgage. And 3 – Small
Business Administration (SBA) Loans. All of these products
possess the features that make a great Inflation Wealth Generator:

their rates are low, fixed and long term.

Cash-Out Refinancing

A Cash-Out Refinance mortgage is a mortgage refinancing option that converts some of your home equity into cash. "Cashing out" is great for investors who are looking for an inflation hedge but do not want to use a mortgage to buy a new home. With a cash-out refinance, a new mortgage larger than what you still owe on your current mortgage is used to pay off the current mortgage.

A portion of the equity you have in your house, usually at least 20% of the new mortgage, functions as the collateral. Any additional equity can be extracted in the form of a loan that equals the value of the home minus the remaining equity used as collateral. It sounds complicated but it is actually straightforward when explained using an example.

Here is how it works:

Suppose Mr. Homeowner has a home valued at $500,000. His current mortgage has a remaining principal of $300,000. He has $200,000 in equity ($500,000 - $300,000 = $200,000). Mr. Homeowner has a problem. He wants to get his hands on the equity he has amassed, but he loves his home and does not want to sell it. Fortunately for him, the cash-out refinancing will allow him to access some of his equity without having to sell his home.

Mr. Homeowner goes to his bank to refinance his mortgage. The bank agrees to lend him $400,000 or 80% of the appraised value of his home ($500,000 x .80 = $400,000). The bank pays off the $300,000 balance of the current mortgage and disburses $100,000 to Mr. Homeowner. His net worth remains unchanged. His liabilities increased by $100,000 because his mortgage balance increased from $300,000 to $400,000, but now he has an extra $100,000 in his checking account. The cash-out refinancing redistributed $100,000 of his home's equity to his checking account.

The cash-out refinancing serves two important functions. First, it serves as an Inflation Wealth Generator. After all, it is just like taking out a home mortgage. The only difference is that the mortgage is on a home you already own. It meets the criteria for our perfect IWG: it is a long-term, low-rate fixed loan on an asset that reliably appreciates at or above the rate of inflation.

Second, a cash-out refinancing allows us to harness the wealth generating power of inflation when it is most powerful – at the beginning of the mortgage term. Recall Graph 3 in Chapter 3, which shows that inflation decreases the real value of debt with the passage of time. However, as time goes on, the amount of the reduction is less and less. This is because the value of the debt has already been made smaller by the previous inflation. The cash-out refinancing resets your IWG to its most profitable setting.

For example, if you had a debt of $100,000 and inflation is 7%, then after Year 1 the value of your debt would have dropped to $93,000. Inflation saved you $7,000 of purchasing power. At the end of Year 2, inflation would have reduced your debt another 7% to $86,490. This time we only saved $6,490 in purchasing power. Every year the amount we "save" because of inflation is less and less.

This makes intuitive sense. If you have a 10% off coupon, then you'll have a bigger absolute savings if you buy something that costs $1,000 ($100 savings) than if you buy something that costs $500 ($50 savings). In the case of a home mortgage, inflation produces the biggest savings when the principal, in nominal and real terms, is largest, which is usually at the very start of the term.

What does this mean in practical terms? It means that you should consider doing a cash-out refinancing as frequently as possible to reap the highest reduction in the value of your debt. And the more you can borrow, the more you will "save." A good rule of thumb when taking out a mortgage or obtaining any type of fixed debt is that if the debt's real interest rate is negative --

that is, if inflation is greater than the debt's interest rate -- then acquiring the debt makes economic sense.

Finally, the cash-out refinancing gives the homeowner tax-free access to their equity. Tax free you say? Since there is no net change in net worth, there is no capital gain and, more important, no capital gains tax. In fact, the interest paid on the mortgage will be tax deductible via the mortgage interest deduction.

Sure, you will have to pay back the loan. But as we have seen in our previous thought experiments, the burden of repayment diminishes with each passing second as inflation devalues our debt. At the end of the mortgage's term the final payment is merely a trifling annoyance. But why would you ever make the final mortgage payment? As long as interest rates are kept at artificially low rates, why not continuously perform cash-out refinancing the moment you achieve adequate equity?

Reverse Mortgage

A reverse mortgage is a type of loan available to homeowners aged 62 years or older, which allows them to convert a portion of their home equity into cash without selling their home. Unlike a traditional mortgage, where the borrower makes monthly payments to the lender, with a reverse mortgage, the lender makes payments to the borrower. The borrower can receive the money in a lump sum, monthly payments, or as a line of credit.

The amount of money that the borrower can receive depends on the equity in their home, their age, the interest rate, and the type of reverse mortgage they choose. The loan does not need to be repaid until the borrower permanently moves out of the home, sells the property, or passes away. At that time, the loan must be repaid in full, usually by selling the home.

In a reverse mortgage, the interest accrues on the amount of money borrowed and is added to the loan balance each month. The borrower is not required to make any payments on the loan, and the interest compounds over time which results in the amount due being significantly higher than the loan amount.

Let's conduct another thought experiment to determine how a reverse mortgage could act as an inflation wealth generator in an inflationary period. We will keep the conditions the same as our previous example.

Meet Papa Joe

Papa Joe is Average Joe's 62-year-old father. Like his son he is an average man who has an average job. Papa Joe would like to retire but social security just isn't enough for him to live on.

Papa Joe does hold one trump card. His home is worth $300,000 and he owns it free and clear. If he could only extract some of the equity out of it, he could leave the rat race behind and finally retire.

Papa Joe could do a cash-out refinancing on his home, but he is worried that he won't have enough income for a mortgage payment. So, he settles on a reverse mortgage which will give him a lump sum of money with no payments until he moves or dies.

Thought Experiment 4

Papa Joe Creates Wealth with a Reverse Mortgage. Moderate Inflation and Negative Real Interest Rates. No Real Home Value Gains.

Initial Conditions: Year 2023

- Inflation = 10%
- Home value and income increase at the exact rate of inflation
- Stock market increases at the exact rate of inflation
- Home Value = $300,000
- Reverse Mortgage Principal $100,00
- Reverse mortgage at 7% APR fixed
- Real interest rate = -3%

Papa Joe applies for a reverse mortgage and gets approved for $100,000 (the younger you are the less you can borrow as a reverse mortgage and vice versa). His interest rate is fixed at 7% until he dies or moves. Since inflation is at 10%, the mortgage's real interest rate is −3%.

Papa Joe's reverse mortgage meets all our requirements for an IWG:

- Low Fixed Interest Rate — the rate is fixed for the life of the loan and is currently negative.
- Long Term - assuming Papa Joe has a long lifespan,
- No Maintenance Requirement for Collateral — Papa Joe's house is the collateral. He will however be expected to maintain it and pay property tax and insurance.
- Preferential Political/Legal Treatment - politicians and judges favor seniors and real estate.
- Preferential Tax Treatment - no taxes since proceeds of the reverse mortgage is seen as debt and not income.

So how did Papa Joe's reverse mortgage work out for him? Let's crunch the numbers to find out. It's important to remember that with a reverse mortgage no interest payments are made. The interest is deferred but added the principle. The borrower then pays interest on the new higher principal. This leads to a compounding effect. The net result is a higher and higher principal balance the longer the borrower lives or stays in the home.

Papa Joe was no fool and didn't fritter away the $100,000 payout from his reverse mortgage. He invested it in a S&P 500 index fund with the intention of drawing down the fund to zero over the next 30 years.

Sadly after 30 years Papa Joe passed away at the ripe old age of 92. During those 30 years of 10% annual inflation, Papa Joe's home increased in price from $300,000 in 2023 to $5,234,821 in 2053 and his mortgage debt increased from $100,000 in 2023 to $811,650 in 2053. Despite his mortgage principal increasing eight-fold, as a percent of the price of the house, the principal decreased from 33.3% to 15.5%.

Because Papa Joe's reverse mortgage had a negative interest rate, his home appreciated at a faster rate than the mortgage principle. In 2023, he had $200,000 in equity after he took out the reverse mortgage and 30 years later, he had $253,486 (in 2023 dollars). After 30 years, he ended up with an additional $53,486 (2023 dollars).

Home Price 2023	Mortgage Debt 2023	% Mortgage to Price
$300,000	$100,000	33.3%

Real Equity = $200,000 (2023 dollars)

Home Price 2053	Mortgage Debt 2053	% Mortgage to Price
$5,234,821	$811,650	15.5%

Nominal Equity = $4,423,171
Real Equity = $253,486 (in 2023 dollars)

But it gets better. Recall Papa Joe invested his reverse mortgage payout in a S&P 500 index fund that kept up exactly with inflation at 10% a year. Over the 30-year period, Papa Joe was able to withdraw a nominal $528,229 in total yearly withdrawals.

When Papa Joe died, he passed his home onto his son, Average Joe, and there was more than enough equity to pay off the balance of the reverse mortgage. Average Joe can either refinance or sell. Suffice it to say, the reverse mortgage was a good investment for Papa Joe. Not only did he leave a valuable legacy for his son, but he also generated a nice supplemental income for himself.

SBA Loans (Small Business Administration Loans)

The Small Business Administration (SBA) offers several loan programs to help small businesses access financing, including fixed-rate loans. Because these loans are backed by the SBA, lenders are able to offer lower interest rates than they would on traditional loans.

The SBA 504 loan is a fixed long-term loan. It is designed to help businesses purchase fixed assets, including land, buildings, and equipment. The loan is structured as a partnership between the borrower, an SBA-approved Certified Development Company (CDC), and a participating lender. The CDC provides 40% of the total project cost, the lender provides 50%, and the borrower provides the remaining 10%. The loan term can be up to 25 years for real estate and up to 10 years for equipment.

SBA loans mostly meet our requirements for an Inflation Wealth Generator:

- Low Fixed Interest Rate - subsidized by the government and therefore lower than market interest rates. The SBA 504 loan is a fixed rate option.
- Long Term - there are terms up to 25 years in some instances.
- No Maintenance Requirement for Collateral
- Preferential Political/Legal Treatment - SBA loans are often restructured if the business gets in trouble especially if there is a widespread economic slowdown. This occurred en masse during the COVID-19 pandemic slow down. Many SBA loans were restructured to a lower rate, longer term, had payments deferred, or were forgiven all together.
- Preferential Tax Treatment - interest on SBA loans are deductible against the business' income.

There are some potential drawbacks to consider when applying for a fixed-rate SBA loan. The application process can be lengthy and require a significant amount of documentation. In addition, borrowers must meet certain eligibility requirements, including size standards and a strong credit history. Finally, borrowers will need to have a down payment of at least 10% of the total project cost for an SBA 504 loan.

Summary

While the 30-year fixed home mortgage may be the undisputed champion of Inflation Wealth Generators, Cash-Out Refinancing, Reverse Home Mortgages, and SBA loans are all excellent IWG alternatives for certain individuals. Unfortunately, in the case of Cash-Out Refinancing and Reverse Mortgages, they are limited to existing homeowners with significant equity. While SBA loans, are limited to profitable business owners with solid credit and strong track record.

Chapter 10

Watch out for deflation

Watch for falling prices!
—Walmart

In the preceding chapters we've seen how the home mortgage is the most effective Inflation Wealth Generator for the common person. If we expect long-term inflation, which I do, then the long-term prospects for our favored IWG are excellent and will produce significant wealth for those who deploy it.

However, as with all investments, there are risks. For the home mortgage, the biggest risks are deflation, contract modification/ nullification, price and rent controls and confiscatory taxes.

All of the risks to our IWG listed above are government-made. Sometimes deflation will be caused by natural disasters, but the vast majority of time the biggest threat to your IWG will be the government. Do not think because you live in the United States that the Constitution will protect you and your wealth?

It did not protect the 120,000 Japanese Americans sent to internment camps during World War II. Nor did it stop FDR from confiscating the citizenry's gold in 1933. And more recently it did not stop the enactment of such obviously unconstitutional laws as the Patriot Act, the Affordable Care Act and the Eviction Moratorium.

When governments get desperate, they do desperate things. Do not expect public outrage, the major media, the courts or a populist politician to protect you, either. We're on our own, folks.

The specter of deflation

Deflation is by far the biggest threat to our IWG and that's the reason I discuss it in some detail here. It is important to understand deflation and its causes. As inflation-powered investors, we should expect intermittent deflation and be positioned to survive it when it inevitably happens. Fortunately for us, there are some very powerful people and institutions, namely the United States government, that are on our side.

Deflation is defined as a decrease in the overall price level. During periods of deflation, on average, the prices of goods and services decline. The price of some items might still increase, but overall prices go down. Just as inflation decreases the purchasing power of the currency, deflation increases the purchasing power of the currency. Basically, as prices fall, a dollar buys more goods and services. Over time, the dollars you earn or save become increasingly more valuable, which is why deflation is great for savers, wage earners, retirees or anyone on a fixed income.

As the cost-of-living decreases, every holder of dollars effectively receives a raise. The mere act of having dollars provides a real positive return. During a period of deflation, you could literally bury your cash for six months and when you dug it up it would buy more than when you buried it.

Deflation sounds pretty awesome, and it is. For the average person deflation lowers their cost of living and makes assets that were once unaffordable, like houses, within reach. At this point, you're probably thinking, "If deflation is so great, then why is the official policy of the Federal Reserve to achieve and maintain an average annual inflation rate of 2%?"

Good question. You have no doubt heard mainstream economists like the Federal Reserve chairman or the U.S. Treasury secretary fretting over the mere possibility of deflation. And it is not just government economists that are terrified of deflation. It is also the Wall Street bankers, the Titans of Tech, the CEOs of every industry, academia, the mainstream media and politicians of every stripe that near unanimously line up against deflation.

Why? Well, it is not because of any mumbo jumbo about a decrease in aggregate demand or some other pedantic nonsense that government economists spew. And truth be told, they could not care less about deflation in the price of toilet paper, eggs or other consumer goods. What the ruling class really fears is price deflation in the real estate, stock and bond markets.

Why? Because deflation of financial assets blows up the whole system. And by that I mean a Great Depression-like financial crisis that would lead to the reordering of the financial and political hierarchy. More on that later, but first we have to understand what causes deflation.

Deflation is caused by three things: 1. Increase in supply. 2. Decrease in demand. 3. Decrease in the money supply.

> **Increases in Supply** – are caused by productivity gains. These are technological advancements that increase the supply of goods and services, which lowers the price. An example of this would be the personal computer industry. Technological advances have made for increasingly more powerful PCs at lower and lower prices. Productivity gains are a healthy and beneficial deflationary force and the reason human society has enjoyed an increasing standard of living generation after generation.
>
> Our IWG investment strategy is not affected by productivity gains save the unlikely event of the development of a new construction method that

dramatically decreases the cost of building a home which would lower the price of existing homes.

Decrease in Demand – is usually the result of a natural disaster or war, which leads to people becoming fearful of their future employment and income prospects, which in turn results in a wide-scale decrease in demand and consumption that leads to deflation in the short run. These shocks to demand can result in sudden and severe drops in the price of financial assets such as real estate and stocks, which can cause insolvency for debtors in these sectors, especially if they have short-term loans.

Ultimately, shocks to demand result in inflation because the disaster that caused the shock also results in the destruction or sidelining of productive capital, which results in a decrease in the supply of goods and services.

Decrease in the Money Supply – Inflation occurs when the money supply increases but the amount of goods and services remains the same – remember Bubba's auction house. The reverse is also true. When there are fewer dollars chasing the same amount of goods and services, prices fall. In our current debt-based fiat monetary system, decreases in the money supply are almost exclusively caused by government action.

In the United States deflation is caused when Congress increases taxes and/or cuts spending. These tax hikes and/or spending cuts take cash out of the system and decrease the money supply. Also, when central banks increase interest rates, they decrease the money supply. This is usually done to correct a previous policy mistake.

A good example of this would be the current interest rate hikes started in 2022 by the Federal Reserve, which were intended to stymie the inflation caused by years of negative real interest rates. Not only can the price deflation of financial assets cause negative equity for the borrower, but it also can cause his interest rate to rise if he has an adjustable-rate loan. This is why having a fixed rate loan is a must-have for an Inflation Wealth Generator.

The only price deflation that seriously affects the IWG strategy is the deflation of financial assets, primarily real estate and stocks. Real estate because that is the asset we are buying with our IWG and the stock market because when the stock market drops it threatens the whole economy. It is the sudden and steep drops, the so-called crashes, in real estate and stock markets that are most dangerous. They are called crashes not just because of their destructive nature but also because of the rapidity of the decline.

The COVID-19-induced stock market panic of 2020 is an example of the rapid deflation of asset prices causing significant contraction of the money supply. In early 2020 the stock market was near record highs, but it began a swift decline after reports that a novel and deadly virus was spreading from Wuhan, China, to Italy and the rest of the globe.

The stock market crashed as it became apparent just how deadly the virus was. The S&P dropped from its Feb. 19, 2020 peak of 3,386 to a low of 2,237 on March 23, 2020. What was more impressive than the absolute size of the drop was the rapidity of it. It plummeted a total of 34% in just a few weeks and it was not uncommon to see daily drops of 10% or 12%. Because the decline was so quick, many margin investors got margin calls and were forced to sell their holdings, causing more price declines and more margin calls.

My sad tale
Unfortunately, I was also humbled by the 2020 stock market crash and was on the receiving end of several of those margin calls. You are probably wondering how a seasoned investor such as myself

ignored my own advice and invested on margin and subsequently lost hundreds of thousands of dollars? Simple. I fell victim to the same cognitive errors that are common among gamblers, speculators and investors alike – early success, overconfidence and the belief that this time it's different.

Starting in 2017, I began trading options on margin in the stock market and, as stated before, you never want to trade on margin. I'll spare you the details of the trades, but basically I was trading options (naked puts) primarily in the energy sector.

I had formulated a strategy that if the price of oil went up, I made a lot of money. If the price stayed level, I made money. And if the price went down, I would still make money. The only circumstance when I would get hurt was from a significant price drop. And I'm not talking about an ordinary bear market. I'm talking about a market crash from a 9/11 type of event.

Things were going great. Borrowing on margin from my broker, I was making much more profit than if I simply bought and held the stocks. To me it seemed like free money because I was making a return on money that wasn't even mine. It was working out great for me – until the COVID-19 pandemic crashed the stock market and took me down with it.

In early 2020 COVID-19 began ravaging China and then Western Europe. People got really sick and a lot of them died. In a vain attempt to slow down the spread of the virus governments around the world began enforcing lockdowns. They mandated closures of schools, big and small businesses, restaurants, parks, even the beaches of California. Concerts and sporting events were cancelled and if workers and businesses did attempt to engage in commerce, they were arrested. Huge swathes of the economy were shutdown.

With a significant number of workers and businesses sidelined, the stock market and the price of oil understandably fell sharply.

Early on in the crisis I did close out some of my riskier positions, but buyers were few and I sold at huge losses. I still felt OK about it, though. The price of oil had not dropped enough to threaten most of my option positions. And since the ones that were in jeopardy were not due to expire for months, I thought I had plenty of time for their prices to recover.

But stock and commodity prices kept sinking. Oil went to zero and then, inconceivably, kept dropping. That's right. The price of a barrel of oil – the life's blood of the economy and the world's most important commodity – went negative. On April 20, 2020, oil hit a low of -$37 a barrel.

My portfolio would have been OK with a 25% to 30% decline in the price of oil over a couple of months, but the price dropped more than 100% in a matter of days. Needless to say, that's when the margin calls started and I was forced to exit my positions at huge losses. All of the profit I had made – and more – was erased seemingly overnight.

But there was no government agency to cry to. No one cared that a leveraged speculator lost a lot of money on risky stock market bets, at least not while millions of people were getting sick and dying or were out of work. There was no one to sue to get my money back. I had signed waivers, initialed acknowledgments and attested to all kinds of terms and conditions. I was an accredited investor with years of experience who got greedy and lost a ton of money. It's a story as old as the stock market.

After the federal government injected trillions worth of stimulus into the economy and the Federal Reserve promised unlimited liquidity and the large-scale purchase of assets, the stock market quickly recovered and rose to new highs in just a couple of months. Ironically, if I hadn't had to make the margin calls when I did, I would have made a tidy profit on my option positions. But that is what happens when you are overleveraged and are forced to sell.

In 2020 was actually the second time I learned the lesson of buying on margin. The first time was in 2001 after the 9/11 terrorist attacks. Let my sad story be a cautionary tale to all leveraged investors. Bouts of deflation can and do happen even in the midst of a significant inflation of the money supply by government.

The stock market crash of 2020 was caused by a once-in-a-lifetime plague and the government over-reaction to it. It would be easy to take comfort in the infrequency of such dire events and convince yourself that the COVID-19 pandemic was an exception, a devastating outlier that won't happen again in our lifetimes.

But former options trader Nicholas Taleb would strongly disagree. In his 2008 bestseller *Black Swan: The Impact of the Highly Improbable* he says that while it's true that unforeseen and unimaginable events like 9/11 and the COVID-19 pandemic only happen once in a lifetime, it's also true there is an infinite number of possible "once-in-a-lifetime disasters."

That means every few years we can expect the once-in-a-lifetime terrorist attack, plague, volcano eruption, super hurricane, mega-drought or any other one of an infinite number of possible natural or man-made catastrophes. It is all but guaranteed that another "once-in-a-lifetime" Black Swan will occur in the immediate 10 years. Hopefully, you won't have margin positions in your stock portfolio. I know I won't. I have learned my lesson for good.

Placing my chips on inflation

We've seen that the profound and sudden deflation of financial assets happens with relative frequent regularity and can be perilous to both the debtor and inflation investor. In fact, there are many highly regarded economists that believe that deflation, not inflation, will prevail in the coming years. I suggest researching the works of financial researcher Harry Dent, the author of *The Great Depression Ahead*, to gain an opposing perspective before you commit significant funds to any inflation hedge strategy.

What do I think? Well, obviously, since I'm writing a book about inflation, I think that inflation will reign in the near future – but with an important caveat. Inflation will continue but it will be peppered with episodes of stinging deflation. The Federal Reserve and U.S. Treasury have the means of stopping inflation dead in its tracks. Raise interest rates and stop printing money, and the inflation problem is solved. But it is not that simple.

Remember why inflation exists in the first place. Politicians like to stay in power and voters like government services that they do not have to pay for with higher taxes. The government prints money to pay for government services and the voters end up paying for them through the inflation tax. This is why the United States is the largest debtor in the history of the world.

The Federal Reserve can stop inflation by raising interest rates, but doing so will cause deflation and a subsequent depression. Don't forget, deflation bankrupts debtors and even mild deflation will bankrupt the United States government. Even a mild increase in the federal funds interest rate will drop federal tax receipts through the floor and make the national debt unserviceable.

When the money-printing stops, the government has no option but to default on its obligations. That means severe cuts in Social Security, Medicare/Medicaid, veterans' benefits, defense spending and every other government program. Basically, if you are getting a check from the federal government, it is going to get a lot smaller and if you are sending a check to the government, it is going to get a lot bigger.

Austerity, the politically correct euphemism for government breaking promises to its citizens, is never popular with the electorate. There is zero constituency for fiscal rectitude. Even congressional members of the now defunct Tea Party reject spending cuts to their sacred government programs.

Imagine the reaction of the Baby Boomers – virtually all of whom vote – when they are told that next month's Social Security check will be cut in half. Or when welfare recipients are told that they will now start receiving their checks every other month. How do you think the bond market will react when Treasury Bill holders are informed that they won't be receiving a coupon payment this quarter?

Make no mistake. Government defaults are coming. They are a mathematical certainty. The question is whether politicians will default honestly by reducing payments to entitlement recipients, retired government workers and veterans and treasury bond holders. Or whether they let inflation do their dirty work on the sly by cutting the purchasing power of government payments to its dependents and creditors.

When politicians break their sacred promises these days, they don't spark a revolution and get the guillotine. The worst that can happen to them – and the best, most realistic scenario for the country – is that they will merely get thrown out of office. Politicians want to stay in power and can only see as far as the next election. It's for this reason that I don't think there will ever be any sustained effort by the government to fight inflation.

Politicians can always find cover by blaming inflation on greedy corporations and landlords or some other rapacious capitalist. Sure, when inflation spirals out of control, politicians and the Federal Reserve governors they choose will make a big show of fighting inflation, and they might even raise interest rates a few times, as the Fed started doing in 2022. But the politicians will back off once the inevitable recession hits and inflation will resume its steady march upward.

Sustained deflation is rare. In the last 65 years, we have had only one year of deflation as measured by the Consumer Price Index. Between 2008 and 2009 the CPI decreased 0.4% – not even half of a percent. But steep deflation can and does occur interspersed between periods of inflation.

Even during the hyperinflation of the Weimar Republic of the early 1920s there were periods of severe deflation that bankrupted overleveraged speculators of gold. This is remarkable considering that the price of an ounce of gold went from 170 marks in 1919 to 87 trillion marks five years later. Even though the leveraged gold speculators were correct that inflation would increase the price of gold astronomically, there were brief bouts of deflation severe enough to wipe out the overleveraged, thus proving correct the old adage that "the market can stay irrational longer than you can stay solvent."

So remember, you might be 100 percent correct about the prospect of high inflation but it won't save you if you are overleveraged. Even if you are using a fixed-rate, long-term mortgage as an inflation hedge, you should expect short periods of deflationary shocks to the stock and real estate markets. If you are able to make your monthly debt payment during the deflationary periods, your Inflation Wealth Generator will reward you handsomely in the long run. But take it from me, the key to surviving deflation is always to **NEVER BE OVER-LEVERAGED.**

· Roger Martinez ·

Chapter 11

What else could go wrong?

Anything that can go wrong, will go wrong.
— Edward A. Murphy, Jr.

One of the many reasons the United States became an economic superpower is its commitment to the rule of law. That means that the judicial system faithfully upholds contracts in a just manner with strict adherence to the law. The contract defines the terms and obligations for the involved parties and spells out the recourse if one party fails to perform. But not all contracts are alike and they can often be changed in ways that can jeopardize our most effective Inflation Wealth Generator, the fixed-rate home mortgage.

Contract Modification/Nullification

In a fixed-rate home mortgage the contract requires the homeowner to make monthly payments to pay back the loan. If he fails to make timely payments, then the bank can foreclose on his house.

But what if the mortgage's fixed interest rate is 3% and inflation is running at 10% or even 15%? Well, as we've stated many times, this is a great deal for the homeowner because inflation steadily eats away at the value of his debt. But it is potentially ruinous for the lender because the homeowner is paying back the bank with dollars that are becoming worth much less in purchasing power than the dollars the bank lent him.

This is a bum deal for the lending bank and every other bank across the nation in the same boat. It is not hard to imagine that a lot of powerful bank presidents and CEOs will use their considerable political influence to have the terms of their mortgage contracts modified.

Maybe the rate is changed from a fixed to adjustable rate. Or maybe instead of being paid back in dollars the contract is changed to be paid back in gold. This has happened before, and I would not be surprised if it happened again.

The best solution to contract modification is to not have a contract that can be modified. If inflation has dramatically increased the price of your house and the remaining principal of your mortgage is relatively small, then it may be prudent to pay off your mortgage early.

Since so much of this book is dedicated to showing how a fixed-rate home mortgage is the most fruitful Inflation Wealth Generator, you are probably confused as to why I am telling you to pay off a mortgage early. It's because the benefit of inflation to you is greater at the beginning of your mortgage when the real value of your debt is largest than at the end of your mortgage.

If inflation has already caused a large reduction in the real value of your debt, then paying off the remainder of your mortgage to avoid any potential modification of your loan agreement might make sense. Once you have the deed to your house, I seriously doubt if there could be any retroactive modification to the terms of your paid-off mortgage.

Rent Controls and Moratoriums

Other risks to our favorite Inflation Wealth Generator are price and rent controls. When inflation hits, it typically hits the things we need the most – food, energy and housing – the hardest. These price hikes caused by inflation are great for your finances if you are using a home mortgage as an inflation hedge.

If you have a conventional 20% down-payment mortgage, then every 1% increase in your home's value means a 5% increase in your equity. Increased home values also mean increased rents. This is great for the landlord who's using a mortgage. Higher rents mean higher profits after paying the fixed mortgage payment. This dynamic is what makes the home mortgage such an effective inflation hedge.

Raising rents obviously makes it easier for the landlord to pay his rental property's mortgage. The problem is that tenants hate higher rents. More accurately, everyone, except landlords, hates higher rents, and there are a lot more tenants than landlords.

And since there are many more voters who are tenants than voters who are landlords, it is predictable that politicians will come down on the side of the tenants. This translates into laws and regulations that are sympathetic to tenants and punitive to landlords.

The most common landlord-hostile policy is rent control. Rent controls typically emerge in coveted locales where rents are high and rising. Think New York City, Los Angeles and San Francisco. Once rents soar in response to inflation, expect to hear a cacophony from tenants' rights groups, poverty advocates, community organizers and the like demanding rent control. They will fiercely lobby their local, state and federal governments for rent control measures.

Another inescapable law of economics is that when a good or service is priced below market it is over-consumed and underproduced. Rent control creates a shortage of rental units and makes all non-rent-controlled housing more expensive. Since real estate developers know they will not be able to charge a market rent because of rent control, they divert their construction projects to friendlier locales where they can maximize their capital's profitability.

The tenants who live in a rent-controlled property might have a lower rent than they would otherwise, but everyone else in the area pays a higher rent. Let's not forget about all of the people who never had the chance to live in these desirable places because of the housing that was never built because real estate developers were discouraged by rent control policies.

The average tenant does not have the economic and financial knowledge to understand that rent control causes higher rents and decreased housing. Therefore, rent control is wildly popular with tenants and the general public. In the best of economic times, rent control is considered essential. In an era of high inflation and soaring rents, it will be considered a human right. Rent control will not be confined to the elite coastal cities, so be prepared for nationwide rent control mandates.

If rent control is enacted, it will most likely cap rent increases. The best preparation for high inflation is to have your rent exceed your fixed-rate mortgage payment and have the rent set at the high end of the range for your property.

If the inflation rate is much greater than the allowable rent increases, your expenses may soon be larger than your revenue and your once profitable property becomes a money suck. The good news is that thanks to inflation your property's value has probably soared in value – but good luck selling it with a rent-controlled tenant.

The most egregious form of rent control in our history was the unconstitutional nationwide moratorium on evictions for nonpayment of rent in 2020. Enacted by the Centers for Disease Control in reaction to the COVID-19 pandemic, the moratorium made paying rent voluntary, so it de facto made the cap on rent $0. This federal moratorium was on top of state and local eviction moratoriums.

Let's call this what it was... The government's confiscation of millions of landlords' properties and their redistribution to the tenants. The confiscation was temporary, but in many cases the financial devastation to landlords will be permanent. It has been over a year since the moratorium was declared illegal and landlords are still struggling to evict their non-paying tenants. In theory, the landlords can sue for rent owed and damages; but, in reality, the best they can hope for is to recover pennies on the dollars.

What is worse than the immorality of the moratorium and even the financial devastation it caused was the lack of outcry from the public. Aside from some landlord blogs and podcasts, the American mainstream media was in full agreement with the moratorium. Despite the obvious illegality of the moratorium, the courts dragged their feet and granted stay after stay.

The U.S. Supreme Court finally ruled that the eviction moratorium was unconstitutional, but even then three justices dissented. This blatant theft of wealth by the government was allowed to occur in a period of low inflation. Imagine how the public and the courts will react in times of high inflation.

As we previously noted, the limitation of real estate as an inflation hedge is that you cannot smuggle it out of the country. You are at the whim of the local authorities, so you better choose where you buy real estate wisely. If you think rent control is politically popular now, just wait until rents start increasing 15% to 20% a year.

Rent control is coming in a big way. As long as rent control is not applied nationwide like the eviction moratorium, there still will be locales ripe for real estate investment. The United States is a big country with plenty of jurisdictions still dedicated to the protection of property rights. When it comes to real estate as an inflation hedge, the old adage remains true: Location, location, location.

Confiscatory Taxes

Supreme Court Justice Oliver Wendell Holmes Jr. is famously quoted as saying, "Taxes are what we pay for a civilized society." I am sure from his point of view this was true. He was a government employee. He was a net tax recipient. His salary, health care and retirement were all dependent on taxes. But what is civilized to the wolf is barbarism to the lamb. Ask a small business owner in the private sector, a net taxpayer, his opinion on taxes. It is probably far different from that of Justice Holmes.

Taxes are used to extract wealth from one group and redistribute it to other groups such as government employees, soldiers, welfare recipients, defense contractors, etc. Getting a check from the proceeds of taxes is the carrot. It's the reason why political movements to tax the rich or corporations have such wide popular support. People know that those tax proceeds will benefit them directly or indirectly, or, at the very least, that their tax burden will decrease as the rich get fleeced.

Taxes can also be used to punish those who happen to be on the wrong side of the current political divide. This is the stick that goes with the carrot. Taxes can be used by the political class in power to confiscate the wealth of those whose profits are deemed undeserving or the result of exploitive practices. These are called "windfall profit taxes."

Windfall profit taxes are typically imposed on sectors of the economy that have had a significant and unexpected increase in value. Politicians will typically threaten oil companies with windfall profit taxes whenever there is a steep increase in oil prices. However, windfall taxes can be placed by politicians on any sector or commodity.

During periods of high inflation, precious metals, real estate, equities, cryptocurrencies, etc., all have the potential to have significant price increases that far outstrip the official rate of inflation.

There will be many detractors who will attribute your foresight in obtaining these assets to luck, or worse, fraud. Therefore, they believe, your newfound wealth is undeserved and a prime target for confiscation and redistribution back to the collective.

Confiscatory tax rates may not even be part of an overt political agenda. They might just be a practical means of raising revenue to pay for the increasing costs of running a huge, sprawling and expensive government. Raising tax rates is also considered to be an inflation-fighting tool by mainstream economists. During high inflation, expect higher rates on property, capital gains and income taxes.

There is not much you can do to lower your property taxes aside from living or investing in low-tax areas. You can lower your income tax by shifting your income from active to passive. You can lower your capital gains taxes by holding your assets for more than a year, because long-term capital gains are taxed at a lower rate than short-term capital gains.

You can also avoid capital gains altogether by not selling your property and instead borrow against it. As far as the IRS is concerned, no capital gains were realized and therefore no taxable event has occurred. I never recommend a margin loan for the reasons mentioned earlier. However, a cash-out refinancing loan may be an effective tax minimization technique and inflation hedge for a homeowner provided you can get a low fixed-rate mortgage for a 15- or 30-year term.

Capital Controls

Capital flows to where it is treated best. If one jurisdiction is not adequately protecting property rights or is actively infringing on property rights, then capital will flow out of that jurisdiction to friendlier locations. Makes sense. If you get mugged every time you walk down a particular street, then unless you are suicidal or nuts you are going to avoid that street.

However, your government is not going to just let you leave the country with your wealth. In fact, you will be lucky if it lets you leave at all. Governments have measures known as "capital controls" that are used to restrict the flow of economic and human capital out of the country. Usually this takes the form of restrictions of international investment, currency exchange and cash withdrawal from banks. In some instances, people with specialized skills who are deemed vital to national interest will be forced to surrender their passports.

Imagine you live in a world in the future where inflation in your country is extremely high with no signs of abating. Fortunately, you have an effective inflation hedge in the form of multiple mortgages that are financing your income-producing rental properties. Everything has worked out just like you figured and planned. The value of your properties soared with inflation and the inflation-adjusted value of your debt plummeted.

But despite your sound financial position, you do not like the direction the country is heading. You can read the writing on the wall. The country, its politicians and its people feel different. They never liked investors and entrepreneurs like you, but it is much worse now.

There is real animosity. You have been labeled a slumlord, a speculator, a price gouger. They say you've gotten rich by exploiting people and you are persona non grata in your own country. Despite being a pillar of the business community, you are being blamed for the country's economic problems. You are getting worried about your investments and your personal safety. It is time to cash out and bug out.

But there is a big problem with leaving your imaginary country. Thanks to the passing of the Economic Freedom and Utopia Act (EF U Act) by Congress, it is now illegal to transfer more than $10,000 annually out of the country.

Also, the EF U Act strictly prohibits purchase of foreign real estate and equities. Exchanging dollars for foreign currency is also illegal. And in case you have any ideas about jacking up your rents to keep pace with inflation, Congress has placed a moratorium on rent increases for the foreseeable future.

Still thinking about leaving to more hospitable foreign shores? Fine. But the exit tax is nearly 100% of your net worth. Failure to comply will result in economic terrorism charges and jail time.

The only legal solution for escaping draconian capital controls like these is to have your capital in friendlier jurisdictions prior to when the controls are enacted. When the guys with guns decide that they want your money, then it is already too late.

It is never a good idea to have all your eggs in one basket. It is always wise to hold some of your wealth outside the country, beyond the grasp of a desperate government. These preparations are outside the scope of this book, but they should include having a second passport, offshore accounts and owning foreign property. If you need them, there are many boutique law and accounting firms that specialize in these services for high net-worth individuals.

If this sounds dystopian or outlandish, or if you think the EF U Act is something I made up because I'm paranoid, then you are probably unaware of what tyrannical lengths politicians will go to stay in power. History is full of examples.

Many historians attribute the rise of Nazism in Germany to the hyperinflation it suffered after World War I. Jews were scapegoated largely because of their economic success. Some Jews left, with their wealth intact, in the early 1930s just as anti-Semitic legislation was getting started. Their friends and families thought they were crazy and being paranoid. But when they realized they were right, it was too late.

Before you send me angry emails accusing me of being some sort of paranoid conspiracy nut, I am not saying the United States government response will be anything like Nazi Germany. Scores of countries have had to deal with high inflation. Some people gain a lot of purchasing power and some people lose a lot of purchasing power. Usually the government will establish a new currency pegged to a more stable currency and austerity measures will be put in place to control government spending. And then life goes on pretty much like before.

Hopefully, in the United States our government's response to high inflation rates will be like Argentina's kinder and gentler response rather than the more brutal response of the Nazis or the socialist thugs running Venezuela today.

In any case, always remember that inflation is a tax and without it politicians are unable to keep their promises and are quickly removed from office or worse. Even the most brutal of dictators will get deposed if they lose the consent of the governed. They will do everything they can to keep the government cash and freebies flowing to their supporters – and that means they need inflation.

Summary

There are an unlimited number of potential threats that can negatively affect the wealth created by our arsenal of Inflation Wealth Generators. Some threats may have not even been conceived of yet, so this list is not meant to be an exhaustive review but rather an overview of the most common hazards:

> **Deflation –** Whether caused by a catastrophic event like the COVID-19 pandemic or political action like tax hikes or spending cuts, it can devastate our preferred leveraged wealth generator, the long-term, low-interest, fixed-rate mortgage. Deflation means a shortage of dollars, making it harder for us to make the interest payments on our debt. We can minimize this risk by limiting our exposure by not overleveraging and by having emergency cash savings to pay our liabilities if sustained deflation occurs.

Contract Modifications/Nullifications – They can occur when our inflation hedges are doing particularly well but public opinion turns against us. The change in the political atmosphere may result in new laws modifying or nullifying our advantageous contract. Consider exiting the contract on your terms before you are forced to accept the less favorable terms of others.

Rent Controls/Moratorium – These will stymie the wealth generated by your investment properties if your rents are not allowed to increase with inflation or, even worse, your rents are not allowed to be collected at all. The trick is to spot the impending legislation (or presidential executive order) that will enact these measures beforehand. Once they are enacted, your only recourse is to unload the property.

Confiscatory Taxes – These are punitive-level taxes that are typically placed on individuals or organizations that are thought to have undeservedly profited from the misery and pain of those who've been hurt by inflation. The public justifies the immorality of these taxes because they are used to punish the greedy slumlord or commodity speculator. Confiscatory taxes are nearly impossible to avoid, short of staying away from investments that you know the public loves to hate. Unfortunately, those despised investments happen to be the best inflation hedges.

Capital Controls – These are severe measures used by desperate governments to keep capital from leaving the country. The best countermeasure for capital controls is to get yourself and your wealth out of the country before the capital controls are enacted.

It should be clear by now that the key is to be able to accurately gauge the political environment and make your financial plans before any of these threats to our Inflation Wealth Generators are enacted. Once they are made law, coping with them is much more difficult. None of us has a crystal ball, but we can sense when the political tide is starting to turn against us. And, in my opinion, it is always better to be a little early than too late.

Chapter 12

Ready for the future

"How did you go bankrupt?"
"Two ways. Gradually, then suddenly."
—Ernest Hemingway, The Sun Also Rises

Congratulations.

You now possess the understanding you need to harness the wealth-generating power of inflation – and you're going to need it.

Although economic trends are not always linear, the reality of our debt-based monetary system guarantees inflation will be in your future. Annual inflation levels may vary, and even periods of deflation can occur, but over the long run inflation will continue unabated. The system relies on it, and the powerful government and corporate stakeholders who profit from a system based on debt will fight any attempt to overturn it.

As I have stated repeatedly, inflation creates winners and losers. It redistributes wealth from creditors and savers to debtors. Since the U.S. federal government holds the dubious distinction of being the largest debtor in history, it has a significant stake in sustaining inflation.

The Federal Reserve has openly expressed its aim to achieve a 2% inflation rate, but it is only a matter of time before the country is engulfed by much higher inflation that will devastate the finances of millions. Throughout history, the political and financial elites have taken advantage of the inflationary policies they have implemented. It is now time for the rest of us to follow suit.

To steer clear of financial ruin caused by inflation, the initial phase involves safeguarding your wealth and purchasing power. Let's review what actions I think you should take, starting with the "Don'ts."

Don't hold or save in dollars. The easiest way to protect yourself from inflation is not to save in cash. Save in something real like precious metals, stocks and real estate. Gold is the best place to store your wealth for the long term. If you cannot afford gold, then save in silver. If you cannot afford silver, then save the way the poor do in the Third World -- by buying the things they need and use. Buy items that have a long shelf life like coffee, liquor, cigarettes, spices, razors, canned goods, etc. These items are easily bartered and if needed consumed.

Don't be a creditor. Another simple way to preserve your purchasing power is not to lend in dollars. This means not buying and holding bonds and not depositing your money in a bank savings account. Remember when you have a savings account, you're actually a creditor of the bank. Not lending money to friends and family is always good advice, even if inflation is zero. By simply avoiding being a saver of dollars or creditor in times of high inflation, you will go a long way to preserving your purchasing power.

Don't invest on margin. A great way of preserving your wealth is simply not to engage in margin loans to invest in the stock market. By not investing on margin, you will save yourself heartache and cash.

Don't invest in annuities. Avoid any investment where you pay a lump sum upfront with the promise to be paid fixed payments in the future. This includes whole life insurance policies. Years of high inflation will significantly reduce the value of these future payments, perhaps even rendering them worthless.

The "Do's" are fewer, but just as simple as the "Don't's."

Do consider taking an early payout of fixed income assets. These include annuities, whole life insurance policies, pensions, structured lawsuit settlements, alimony and child support.

Do consider drawing your Social Security and/or pension as early as possible. High inflation will dramatically reduce the purchasing power of both your Social Security and pension. If you have the option to draw your Social Security or pension early, seriously consider it. Don't make the mistake of waiting too long to cash in your chips.

Generating Wealth and Purchasing Power

Generating wealth and increasing your purchasing power during high inflation takes a little more effort and risk. It requires the use of inflation hedges and the best inflation hedges are deemed Inflation Wealth Generators (IWGs).

In my opinion, as I have stressed, the best IWG is the 30-year-fixed home mortgage. It meets all our requirements for an IWG: Low Fixed Interest Rate, Long Term, No Maintenance Requirement for Collateral, Preferential Political/Legal Treatment and Preferential Tax Treatment.

The 30-year-fixed-home mortgage will generate significant wealth for you and all you need to do is be patient and make your monthly payment. Once you have enough equity, you can use cash-out refinancing to extract a portion of the equity tax-free. Once inflation has increased the price of your home and you have enough equity to qualify, then refinance it again. Rinse and repeat. It is really that simple.

Protecting Your Wealth

Protecting your wealth once you have earned it is the final step to becoming a successful inflation-powered investor. Because inflation is a government-made phenomenon, the government is always the greatest threat to your wealth, regardless of whether it was created through inflation or by another means.

The greatest catastrophe that can befall an Inflation Wealth Generator is deflation. It could come in the form of a Black Swan event like the COVID-19 pandemic, or some other once-in-a-lifetime disaster. Or it could be the result of a monetary or fiscal action taken by the federal government to fight inflation.

Regardless of the cause of deflation, however, the prescription is the same and that is never to be overleveraged. It doesn't matter if deflation is Fed-made or an act of God, if you are not overleveraged and have a steady income you will survive even the most stubborn bouts of deflation.

Other threats to your wealth are also political in nature and occur when governments stop protecting and start infringing on your property rights. These include contract modification/nullification, rent control/moratorium, confiscatory taxes and capital controls.

There are strategies mentioned earlier to mitigate these threats. One strategy is paying off your Inflation Wealth Generator after it has produced the bulk of its profit and before contract modifications take place. Also, utilizing a cash-out refinancing is a great way to minimize your tax burden.

But the most important thing to realize is that all these political threats to your wealth are just variations of property rights violation.

Unfortunately, once a government starts infringing on your rights, the trend is typically for more and more infringements until there is a revolutionary event that sends the pendulum swinging back in the opposite direction.

To paraphrase Ernest Hemingway, "Nations, like men, go bankrupt slowly and then all at once." The United States is rapidly approaching the "all at once" phase. So, what does the future look like?

An inflationary crisis doesn't necessarily mean we face a dystopian "Mad Max" future with Americans fighting each other in the streets for rat meat. Scores of countries have suffered through decades of rampant inflation and have managed to get by. For example, the people of Argentina have lived with extremely high inflation for most of their lives.

In 2022 alone their inflation rate was 95% and yet life went on as normal for most Argentines. Make no mistake. Inflation is a terrible burden, but don't cry for the people of Argentina. They're not starving. Their life expectancy is comparable to people living in the United States -- and they just won the 2022 FIFA World Cup.

But inflation is a heavy and ubiquitous tax. All taxes create inefficiencies and misallocations of resources that can hold back a country's progress and hold down its standard of living. Runaway inflation in Argentina since the early 1900s has severely hampered its economic growth.

The country was almost as rich as the United States at the start of the 20th century. But in the 1930s a succession of bad government policies led to chronic government over-spending and currency defaults. Today, Argentina is solidly a Third World country with a per capita income at about the same level as Mexico.

Predicting the future?

So what do I think is in store for the USA? First, I do not think we will return to the gold standard in the near term. Only hyperinflation will create a constituency powerful enough to demand sound money. Nor do I think the Federal Reserve or the nation could endure the prolonged interest-rate-hiking campaign that would be necessary to fight inflation. At least not with the present $32 trillion national debt and the huge interest payments we already must pay on it each year.

I predict we will have a decade's worth of moderate inflation – between 5% and 10% annually. Ten years of inflation at 7% cuts the real value of the national debt in half and probably doubles nominal GDP.

Then, suddenly, the United States' balance sheet starts looking a whole lot better. At that point the Federal Reserve could mount a serious fight against inflation like the one Federal Reserve Chairman Paul Volker did in the early 1980s when he raised interest rates to 20%.

But while the federal government would see its massive debt halved after a decade of 7% inflation, the pensioner would see the purchasing power of his monthly payment cut in half and the bondholder would see the real value of his principal cut in half.

Tragically, hundreds of millions of Americans would become casualties from ten years of high inflation, but not you. That's because whether your goal is early retirement, financial freedom, travel or philanthropy, you now possess the knowledge to design your own Inflation Wealth Generator, reverse your financial trajectory and enrich your life.

Appendix

Price of Silver Over 100 Years
with 7% Annual Inflation Rate
Table 1

Year	Price	Year	Price	Year	Price	Year	Price
0	$25.00	26	$145	52	$843	78	$4896
1	$ 26.75	27	$155	53	$902	79	$5239
2	$ 28.62	28	$166	54	$965	80	$5606
3	$ 30.63	29	$178	55	$1033	81	$5998
4	$ 32.77	30	$190	56	$1105	82	$6418
5	$35.06	31	$204	57	$1183	83	$6867
6	$ 37.52	32	$218	58	$1265	84	$7348
7	$ 40.14	33	$233	59	$1354	85	$7863
8	$ 42.95	34	$249	60	$1449	86	$ 8413
9	$ 45.96	34	$267	61	$1550	87	$ 9002
10	$ 49.18	36	$286	62	$1659	88	$ 9632
11	$ 52.62	37	$306	63	$1775	89	$10306
12	$ 56.30	38	$327	64	$1899	90	$11028
13	$ 60.25	39	$350	65	$2032	91	$11800
14	$ 64.46	40	$374	66	$2174	92	$12625
15	$ 68.98	41	$401	67	$2326	93	$13509
16	$ 73.80	42	$429	68	$2489	94	$14455
17	$ 78.97	43	$459	69	$2663	95	$15467
18	$ 84.50	44	$491	70	$2850	96	$16549
19	$ 90.41	45	$525	71	$3049	97	$17708
20	$ 96.74	46	$562	72	$3263	98	$18947
21	$103.51	47	$601	73	$3491	99	$20274
22	$110.76	48	$643	74	$3735	100	$21693
23	$118.51	49	$688	75	$3997		
24	$126.81	50	$736	76	4277		
25	$135.69	51	$788	77	$4576		

Amount of Silver $100 Can Purchase at 7% Inflation
(Table 2)

Year	Ounces	Year	Ounces	Year	Ounces	Year	Ounces
0	4	26	0.78858	52	0.13579	78	0.02042
1	3.73832	27	0.73699	53	0.12690	79	0.01908
2	3.49375	28	0.68878	54	0.11860	80	0.01783
3	3.26519	29	0.64372	55	0.11084	81	0.01667
4	3.05158	30	0.60160	56	0.10359	82	0.01558
5	2.85194	31	0.56225	57	0.09681	83	0.01456
6	2.66536	32	0.52546	58	0.09048	84	0.01360
7	2.49099	33	0.49109	59	0.08456	85	0.01271
8	2.32803	34	0.45896	60	0.07903	86	0.01188
9	2.17573	35	0.42893	61	0.07386	87	0.01110
10	2.03339	36	0.40087	62	0.06902	88	0.01038
11	1.90037	37	0.37465	63	0.06451	89	0.00970
12	1.77604	38	0.35014	64	0.06029	90	0.00906
13	1.65985	39	0.32723	65	0.05634	91	0.00847
14	1.55126	40	0.30582	66	0.05266	92	0.00792
15	1.44978	41	0.28582	67	0.04921	93	0.00740
16	1.35493	42	0.26712	68	0.04599	94	0.00691
17	1.26629	43	0.24964	69	0.04298	95	0.00646
18	1.18345	44	0.23331	70	0.04017	96	0.00604
19	1.10603	45	0.21805	71	0.03754	97	0.00564
20	1.03367	46	0.20378	72	0.03509	98	0.00527
21	0.96605	47	0.19045	73	0.03279	99	0.00493
22	0.90285	48	0.17799	74	0.03065	100	0.00461
23	0.84378	49	0.16635	75	0.02864		
24	0.78858	50	0.15546	76	0.02677		
25	0.73699	51	0.14529	77	0.02501		